A Stage for the King

A Stage for the King

THE TRAVELS
OF CHRISTIAN IV OF DENMARK
AND THE BUILDING OF
FREDERIKSBORG CASTLE

Patrick Kragelund

MUSEUM TUSCULANUM PRESS

Patrick Kragelund, *A Stage for the King:*
The Travels of Christian IV of Denmark
and the Building of Frederiksborg Castle

2019 © Museum Tusculanum Press and Patrick
Kragelund
Layout, composition and cover design: Pernille Sys
Hansen / Damp Design
Set in Kis Antiqua Now TH, which is a digital interpretation of Miklós Kis' type designs, made during
his stay in Amsterdam in the late 1600s.
Printed on Arctic Volume White 130 g in Denmark by
Tarm Bogtryk
ISBN 978 87 635 4594 5

The production of this volume is generously
supported by:
15. Juni Fonden
E. Lerager Larsens Fond
Landsdommer V. Gieses Legat
Lillian og Dan Finks Fond
Ny Carlsbergfondet

No part of this publication may be reproduced,
stored in a retrieval system, or transmitted in any
form or by any means, electronic, mechanical, photocopying, recording, or otherwise without the prior
written permission of the publishers.

Distrubuted in the UK and Ireland by
Gazelle Book Services.
Distributed in Scandinavia by
Museum Tusculanum Press.
Distributed in North America and the rest
of the world by
the University of Chicago Press.

Museum Tusculanum Press
Dantes Plads 1
1556 Copenhagen V
Denmark

www.mtp.dk

Contents

	Preface	6
I	Introduction: "Nowhere in the Country…"	11
II	The Forecourt, the Terrace and the Gateway	21
III	Theobalds, and After	31
IV	The Marble Gallery	61
V	The Seven Planet-Gods	87
VI	Jupiter *and the King*	109
VII	The Royal Tiltyard and the Imperial Palace of Rome	117
ENVOI	Palatial Settings for a "Ceremonial Court"	161
	Notes	169
	Bibliography	183
	Summary in Danish	191
	Index of Places, Monuments and Persons	195
	Image credits	199

Preface

Frederiksborg is a monument in the World Heritage class, and it has been a privilege to work on it. Many have helped locating known and, in several happy cases, overlooked sources of relevance for understanding the castle as it once was. Thanks to staff of the Danish Academy in Rome, the Library of the Warburg Institute, the Bibliotheca Hertziana in Rome and the National Art Library at the Victoria and Albert Museum in London, the Royal Danish Collections at Rosenborg, the National Museum of Denmark, the Museum of National History at Frederiksborg and my former place of employment, the Danish National Art Library.

I would like to express my gratitude to the following individuals for lending kind support in the preparation of this publication: architects Kent Alstrup and Mette Marciniak of the Danish Heritage authority Slots- og Kulturstyrelsen for inviting me to lecture, for giving me a tour of the Frederiksborg Marble Gallery under restoration and for giving access to Frederiksborg's *Lapidarium*, Dr Nan Dahlkild and Dr Vibeke Andersson-Møller for inviting me to lecture at the Society of History of Architecture, Dr Peter Zeeberg for inviting me to lecture at our old debating society, Filologisk-Historisk Samfund, Dr Ann Benson for sharing her knowledge of Queen Anne and establishing contact to the Enfield Archaeological Society, Dr Martin Dearne, Mr. Ian Jones and Mr. Michael Dewbrey of the Enfield Archaeological Society for showing me the archaeological remains of Theobalds on a cold, but sunny January morning, Dr Paula Henderson and Dr Claire Gapper for inviting me to lecture at a meeting in the Society of Antiquaries in London in January 2017, Dr Emily Cole, English Heritage, for sharing her knowledge of court ceremonial and of Theobalds and to Paul Backhouse, Head of Imaging, English Heritage, for generously allowing me to reproduce the splendid new reconstruction of the castle's exterior (fig. 3.8). I furthermore owe an invaluable debt to the following: Dr Julie Farguson for inviting me to a conference on Danish Royal Consorts at Queen's House, Greenwich, my niece, the architect, MAA Kirsten Marie Kragelund for drawings and measurings, Dr Cay Dollerup for letting me consult his transcript of a diary from Cristian IV's visit to England in 1606, Dr Per Seesko at the Museum of National History at Frederiksborg for help with an inscription (ch. IV, n. 11), Professor Konrad Ottenheym, Utrecht, for help with Dutch originals, Dr Peter Kristiansen at the Royal Danish Collections at Rosenborg, Dr Marie Martens at The Danish Music Museum for precious information about a portrait of King Christian (fig. 4.10) and a group of the king's musicians (fig. 8.1), and, finally, the Christian IV experts (and old friends) Dr Steffen Heiberg, previously at Frederiksborg, and Dr Jørgen Hein, at the Royal Danish Collections at Rosenborg, for their unfailing support.

For defraying the costs of study visits abroad as well as production, I am deeply indebted to the Ny Carlsbergfondet for supporting visits to Dresden and London and for meeting the costs of illustrations; the 15. Juni Fonden, E. Lerager Larsens Fond, Landsdommer V. Gieses Legat and Lillian og Dan Finks Fond have made it possible to produce a book of such high quality. Please receive my sincerest thanks for this generous vote of confidence!

My publishers, thankfully, believed in the project from day one. My partner, Dr Mogens Nykjær, never failed in putting frustrating setbacks into a humorous perspective.

"Nicht Zeit ist's mehr, zu brüten und zu sinnen,
Denn Jupiter, der glänzende, regiert
Und zieht das dunkel zubereitete Werk
Gewaltig in das Reich des Lichts – Jetzt muss
Gehandelt werden, schleunig, eh die Glücks-
Gestalt mir wieder wegflieht überm Haupt,
Denn stets in Wandlung ist der Himmelsbogen."

Friedrich Schiller, *Wallensteins Tod* 1.1.

"The time is o'er of brooding and contrivance,
For Jupiter, the lustrous, lordeth now,
And the dark work, complete of preparation,
He draws by force into the realm of light.
Now must we hasten on to action, ere
The scheme, and most auspicious positure
Parts o'er my head, and takes once more its flight.
For the heavens journey still, and sojourn not."

Wallenstein's Death 1.1, translated by Samuel T. Coleridge

FIG. 1.1. Melchior Lorck, portrait of King Frederik II of Denmark & Norway. Engraving from 1582, 45 × 32. The National Gallery of Denmark.

In 1560 King Frederik acquired the area and castle to the north of Copenhagen, which he renamed Frederiksborg. As soon as his son and successor came of age, Christian IV pulled down his father's residence, but out of piety he retained its old name. It was only in 1730, when his great-great grandson, Christian VI pulled down the ancient Copenhagen Castle and renamed its successor Christiansborg, that the dynasty's by then six Christians, from the founder onwards, were similarly honoured.

I

Introduction: "Nowhere in the Country…"

FIG. 1.2. *Christian IV painted by Pieter Isaacsz*, 1612, oil on canvas, 140 × 106. The Museum of National History at Frederiksborg.

Flamboyant and lavish, Christian IV (1577–1648) raised the Danish monarchy up to hitherto unseen peaks of luxury and extravagance. A great builder and founder of new cities, a devout Christian, heavy drinker, music lover and womaniser, the splendour of his court has, despite the military catastrophes at the end of his reign, given him an affectionate place in the popular historical imagination, the so-called Rosenborg style (in fact Dutch Renaissance) becoming an emblem of Danishness in the late nineteenth century. The portrait's almost tactile and glittering qualities, from silks and brocades and from gold and jewellery, are characteristic of the period's aesthetic. So is the panegyric equation between the king and the victorious Roman emperor returning in triumph (on the marble pedestal carrying the crown). This Greco-Roman dimension to the king's imagery is central to this book.

IN THE DECADES BETWEEN 1602 AND 1622 THE Danish and Dutch sculptors and master builders of Denmark & Norway's King Christian IV (fig. 1.2) furnished the new royal residence at Frederiksborg with an unprecedentedly rich and varied sculptural decoration.

Fountains, arches and groups of freestanding sculptures were ordered from artists at home and abroad, such as Adriaen de Vries (1545–1626) in Prague, Hendrick de Keyser (1565–1621) in Amsterdam and Hans van Steenwinckel the Younger (1587–1639) in Denmark, to adorn the castle facades and courtyards, as well as its Tiltyard. And these in such numbers and magnificence that one can easily understand the baffled reactions not only of contemporaries,[1] but also of later generations. As an early nineteenth-century antiquarian observes: "What astonishes about this castle is that nowhere in the country can one find a larger decorative assembly of figures and ancient statues adorning a single building than here".[2] "Nowhere in the country" – nor, indeed, in Scandinavia – would a seventeenth-century visitor be welcomed by such a grand gathering of the gods of Olympus. All counted, there were more than sixty such statues in bronze or sandstone, mostly life-size. In Denmark, the typical Renaissance emphasis on the monarch's links to Greece and Rome (fig. 1.3) had of course been introduced at Kronborg Castle in Elsinore under King Frederik II (fig. 1.4). But under his son, it reached its fullest Nordic blossoming.[3]

For an educated seventeenth-century visitor the sheer sight of this assembly would have given cause for delight. The sculptural mastery, the use of black and red sandstone and the extensive use of gilding were easy to appreciate. Stories of the cost of it all would have added to its prestige – and sometimes constituted the object of predominant interest. But an envoy or princely guest would, just as much as a humanist spectator, also be on the lookout for coherence and ingenuity in combining old and familiar symbols and myths in a manner suitable for a royal residence. Under the king's father, Frederik II, such awareness was already well established. In his epic on female power dedicated to England's Queen Elizabeth, the court poet Erasmus Laetus would, in true Renaissance fashion, furnish his fictional council chamber of Medieval Queen Margrethe I of Denmark, Norway & Sweden with paintings featuring Biblical and mythological heroines, all mirroring the queen's qualities.[4] For Christian IV, his humanist advisors and learned chancellors[5] there would have been no doubt that the decoration of his new castle demanded detailed planning. Given the sheer scale of the endeavour and the art historical importance of the result, it is worth the while to examine what one can – despite the havoc caused by time, replacements and, worst of all, the restorative interventions following the catastrophic fire in 1859 – bring to light about the original layout of this grandiose sculptural programme as well as about the way the castle's architecture was adjusted to meet these aesthetic demands (fig. 1.5). Far from merely being adornments added onto the existing architecture, these sculptures were in fact often decisive in determining how the castle was ultimately designed and its exterior fashioned (fig. 1.6).

In order to uncover the original appearance of the castle, this book combines the unravelling of – at times hitherto discarded – visual and written contemporary evidence with the deciphering of the imagery that visitors would have seen in the days of King Christian IV. By this approach it presents a, in crucial respects,

FIG. 1.3. Painted trophies by Samuel Clausen from King Christian's study at Rosenborg, Castle, 1617, oil on canvas, 79.2 × 20.1 and 79.4 × 20. The Royal Danish Collection, Rosenborg. To the left Rome with a banner inscribed SPQR (*Senatus Populusque Romanus*/"The Roman Senate and People"), to the right Denmark & Norway with the king's motto RFP, i.e. REGNA FIRMAT PIETAS ("Piety strengthens the Realms"). In the king's sad final years, the motto was wittily parodied: "The Realm needs Money" (*Riget Fattes Penge*).

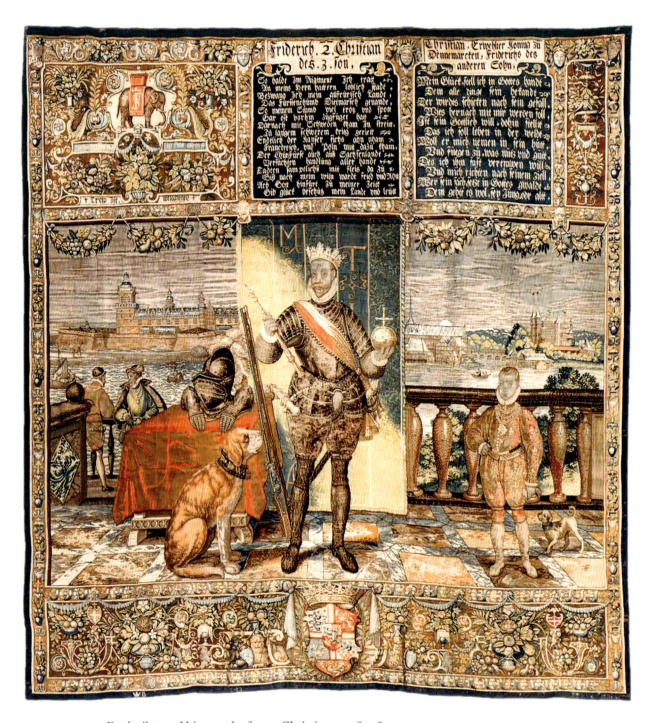

FIG. 1.4. Frederik II and his son, the future Christian IV, 1582–84, 394 × 367. The National Museum of Denmark.
The final of the originally forty tapestries depicting the one hundred Danish kings since the legendary King Dan (cf. fig. 4.11). The tapestries were woven by Hans Knieper for the Great Hall at Kronborg in Elsinore. Visible behind King Frederik II is his magnificent Kronborg at Elsinore, behind Crown Prince Christian his birthplace Frederiksborg, as it looked in his childhood.

completely new reading of Frederiksborg's decorative programme. At a juncture of time when an ambitious and costly restoration of the castle's Marble Gallery is being planned by the Danish government's Agency for Castles and Culture (SLKS), it is to be hoped that these new insights will enable future interventions to avoid repeating the errors of the past.

As for the castle's architecture there are likewise crucial aspects to reassess. The compound is a visual marvel. The richness of its décor and the vast, impressive symmetry of the group of buildings, which straddle three islands and have an uninterrupted sightline reaching from the S-bridge and towering Gate-House across the Forecourt all the way up to the facade of the Royal Wing, is in the sheer length of its fully frontal, linear approach a complete novelty in North European architecture. Nowhere in Scandinavia is there in this period a similarly expansive, some 120 metres long "straight-as-an-arrow" approach to a building complex of an equally symmetrical disposition. But when and by whom was this expansive deployment thought out? Was there a comprehensive masterplan from the very beginning? Or was this masterplan something that only after some false starts gradually came to be adopted? As will be laid bare, there are in fact clear signs that plans at some point were changed, from an at first very traditional mould to something very innovative. And as we shall see, the inspiration for this pioneering and innovating approach reaches beyond architectural treatises (which commonly have been quoted as models) to palatial architecture actually seen and admired during the king's visits to Dresden in 1597 and, above all, to England in the summers of 1606 and 1614.

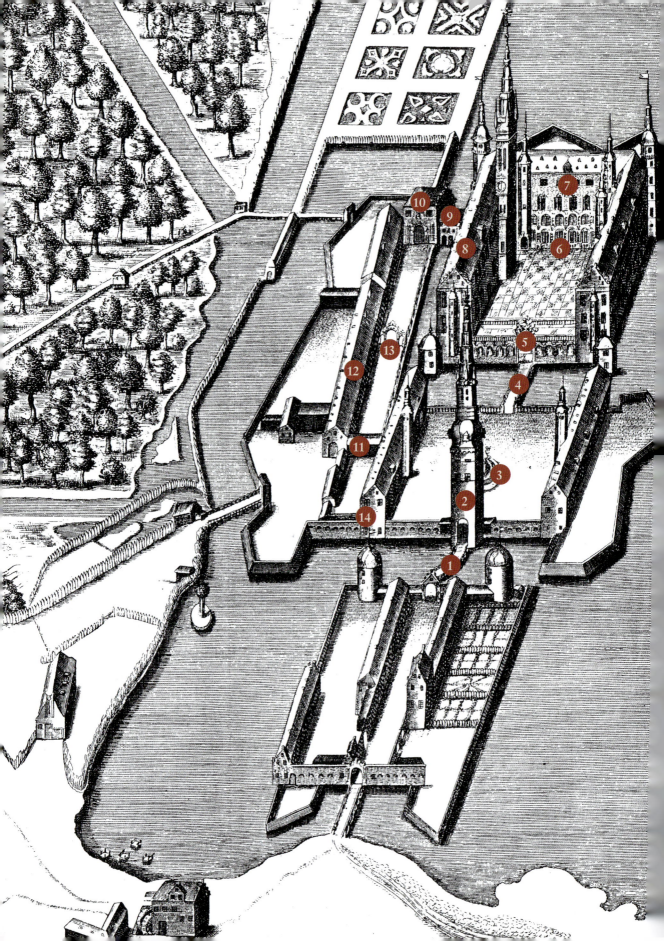

FIG. 1.5. Frederiksborg. A bird's-eye view from 1646 reproduced in Berg's *Beschreibung* from that year. Danish National Art Library. North is upwards. The added numbers refer to monuments discussed in this study: 1 The S-bridge. 2 The Gateway Tower. 3 The Neptune fountain. 4 The bridge across the moat. 5 The Terrace. 6 The Inner Courtyard's Marble Gallery. 7 The Royal Wing. 8 The Chapel Wing. 9 The Privy Gallery. 10 The Audience House. 11 The *Judicirhaus*/ "Judges' House" (pulled down in 1865). 12 The Kitchen and Stables wing. 13 The Arch for running at the ring competitions. 14 The House of the Master of the Castle.

FIG. 1.6. Bird's-eye view of Frederiksborg.

FIG. 2.1. Lazarus Baratta, *Frederiksborg*, 1652, oil on canvas, 205 × 208. It was painted for Frederik III (riding in the foreground) but taken to Sweden as war booty. Now kept at Gripsholm Castle in Sweden.

II

The Forecourt, the Terrace and the Gateway

THE FIRST IMPRESSION IS MESMERIZING (fig. 2.2). When seen from the semiumbra beneath the majestic Gateway Tower and with the entire castle facade as the resplendent background, the lower, more sparingly decorated buildings of the Forecourt create a crescendo of impressions that in an inverted perspective leads forwards and onwards to the fully frontal view of the three-winged residence, which with its multi-colour elevation, curving gables and soaring copper spires measures some 65 metres from east to west.

The overall impression is highly ornate, the red-brick facades adorned with horizontal sandstone bands, the top gables with towering obelisks. The whole speaks clearly of the impact of Dutch and German renaissance architecture. The swung gables and steep obelisks are for instance right out of pattern books by Hans Vredeman de Vries, whereas much of the decorative strapwork detail draws upon the inventions of Wendel Dietterlin. Up the middle of the gables, the richly carved oriels that reach from the ground almost to the top add to the festive magnificence. The emphasis on symmetry is heavily in evidence. Indeed, the western (left) oriel is mainly decorative, the window at the top in fact a fake. Just behind it, the imposing chimney piece of the Great Hall blocks what from the outside seems a window.

To strengthen the majestic impact of symmetry, the centre Forecourt was in 1620–22 provided with a multi-figure Neptune fountain created by the imperial sculptor Adriaen de Vries. The glittering multi-figure (originally gilded) bronze fountain is a visual triumph that splendidly animates the impact of the architecture framing the Forecourt and Inner Court, even in the eyes of art historical connoisseurs fully

FIG. 2.2. Frederiksborg. The Forecourt with Adriaen de Vries' reconstructed Neptune fountain.

aware that this is a nineteenth-century reconstruction. In its reconstructed form, the fountain reassembles casts from the originals now on display in the gardens of Drottningholm Palace outside Stockholm.[1] It is crowned by Neptune, the Lord of the Ocean, whose arm is raised majestically high in a gesture of greeting and command, while symbols of the seas surrounding

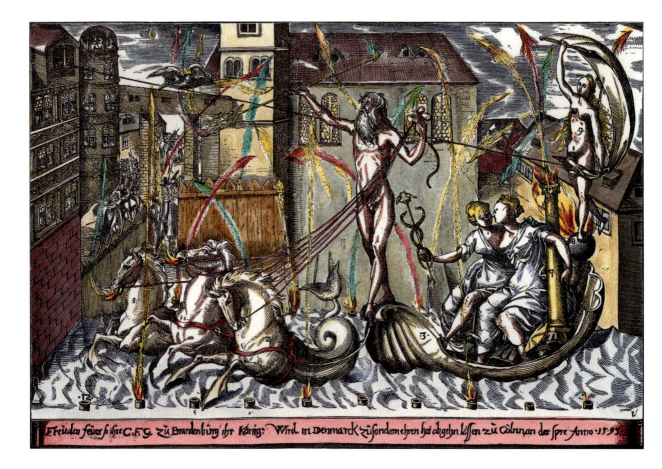

the monarch's realms encircle the pediment to his feet. Three river-gods pour water into the fountain, as do three Tritons, while three goddesses, Venus, Ceres and, probably, Ariadne, embody the blessings of fertility. These are perhaps the finest sculptures of the castle, specimens of elegant, ultimately Florentine, mannerism far to the north.

The fountain's classical imagery serves as a sculptural prelude to what follows on the facades of the Terrace and the Royal Wing, with their two times twelve ancient gods and heroes – but more on that later. What matters here is that the fountain's linking of the king and Neptune was an oft-repeated element in the period's royal panegyric,[2] an element that was

FIG. 2.3. A firework display set off in honour of the visit of Christian IV in Berlin 1595. The engraving is ascribed to Ph. Uffenbach. The colouring is later. Already at this point, a link between the young king and Neptune, the master of the sea, was suggested.

FIG. 2.4. A bowl from the collections of King Christian's eldest son and heir. Milan 1580, gold, enamel, gems and pearls, height 14.7 cm. Grünes Gewölbe, Staatliche Kunstsammlungen, Dresden. The *Dauphin* ("Heir-to-the-throne") symbolism of the dolphin is here wittily combined with the paternal Neptune imagery.

made explicit here by the three lions of the royal coat of arms as well as by the royal ciphers originally held high by the fountain figures of Fame, Victory and Mercury patrolling the marble encasement of the fountain itself.[3] Right at the entrance to the castle's ceremonial Forecourt, this direct linking of the king and of Neptune (fig. 2.3–4) introduces a double rhythm that runs through most of the castle's imagery. Ancient Olympus has its resplendent mirror image in the court of Denmark & Norway.

II · THE FORECOURT, THE TERRACE AND THE GATEWAY 25

The fountain's evocation of the king's *dominium* of the Baltic (a slogan from 1638 describing the aim of his lifelong policy)[4] is then, as the visitor moves forward, supplemented by images of the ancient universal empires, here represented by Alexander the Great and Julius Caesar, each standing high on a pair of columns framing the entrance to the bridge spanning the castle moat (fig. 2.5).

According to the account of the Castle Guardian published in 1646, it is Alexander who guards the bridge on its eastern side, Caesar on the western. This disposition is not coincidental. The conquests of Alexander reached eastwards, all the way to the banks of the Ganges, whereas Caesar brought the Roman eagles across the Channel (or the Ocean, as the Romans called it), to Britain far in the west.[5]

FIG. 2.5. Frederiksborg. The Forecourt with bridge spanning the moat and flanked by columns crowned by statues of Alexander the Great and Julius Caesar (detail from fig. 3.14). The columns and statues are early twentieth-century reconstructions.

FIG. 2.6. *Plvs vltra*. The device of the Emperor Charles V. From M. Claude Paradin, *Princelijcke Devijsen ofte wapenen*, Antwerp 1562, 18.

This programmatic display, originally with near life-size gilded[6] statues on top of the Tuscan columns, would in the eyes of contemporaries speak clearly of power and ambition. In a pictorial language evoking the famous Herculean device of the emperor Charles v (fig. 2.6), this double column symbolism is panegyric hyperbole, alluding to power reaching far and wide, from sunrise to sunset (the period's ruler panegyric was characterised by neither modesty nor realism).[7]

At the end of the bridge, on the richly decorated threshold to the castle's Inner Courtyard, heraldic lions stand guard. They were renewed in the early twentieth century. The originals were hewn from alabaster, a choice giving the ensemble a remarkable variety of colour, from red-brick and sandstone to lucid marble and glittering gold. Above the portal, the (originally painted and gilded) coats of arms of the king (left) and queen (right) are crowned by the cipher of Christian IV and on top of the gable diminutive statues of Minerva (left) and Diana (right) frame a Jupiter with the eagle (fig. 2.7). This motif with the king of the gods as the top figure is, as we shall see, to be repeated and brought to a triumphant culmination in the array of statues crowning the Inner Courtyard's Marble Gallery. But before addressing the questions raised by this final component in the exterior decoration of the castle (chs. IV–VI) a closer look at the architecture and sculptures of the low, one-storey Terrace that spreads out on either side of the bridge and castle entrance is called for (fig. 3.14).

FIG. 2.7. The insignia of King Christian and his queen, Anna Katherina of Brandenburg. Print after drawing by Charles Christensen and Asger Jeppesen, 1917. Danish National Art Library.

The woodwoses flanking the king's coat of arms are traditional, the matching pair of unicorns flanking the arms of the queen are unparalleled in her family's heraldry (as my learned colleague Dr Niels Bartholdy at the National Archives kindly informs me); they are probably here for the sake of symmetry and may well allude to the queen's virtue. The insignia were originally coloured and gilded. Above the shields is a diminutive Jupiter with eagle.

FIG. 3.1. King Christian's Garter robes, which he wore at Windsor in August 1606, when he was given the Order of the Garter during his visit. When the king died in February 1648, Britain was in the middle of a civil war, so nothing came of plans to return the robes and garter. Apparently, this is the oldest surviving example of this ceremonial garb. The Royal Danish Collection, Rosenborg.

III

Theobalds, and After

T**HE TERRACE (NAMED AFTER THE FRENCH** *en terrace*) that connects the castle's two side wings and divides the Forecourt from the Inner Courtyard is architecturally speaking an afterthought. In fact, it replaces a forerunner, barely ten years older, following the decision, in 1619, that this should be pulled down. We know from a painting by Pieter Isaacsz what this more old-fashioned "fortress" wall looked like in c.1615 (fig. 3.2).[1] Its replacement with a modern, French-style terrace is only one among several aspects illustrating how the building project from mid-1606 onwards completely changed direction, a change that deeply affected the castle's whole layout and present appearance.

In terms of chronology, the first clear sign of this dramatic change in ambition and direction is the sudden decision, in September 1606, to add considerably to the height of the Castle Chapel, a decision resulting

FIG. 3.2. Detail from a portrait probably by Pieter Isaacsz of King Frederik III as a child showing Frederiksborg as it looked in c.1615, oil on canvas, 139 × 108. The Museum of National History at Frederiksborg. The wall dividing the Forecourt from the Inner Court is at this point unadorned. In playful imitation of a fortification, it has circular wall-openings for cannons. The flat-roofed terrace gateway, the loggia and twelve statues were only added by van Steenwinckel in 1619.

in a conspicuous clash between the new Chapel Wing and the by then already completed Royal Wing (fig. 3.3). This clash of facades tells of original plans for a somewhat lower chapel, much as in the Kronborg of his father Frederik II. Because of this new dimensioning, the Great Hall which lies above was, as it were, pushed upwards considerably, right up under the roof. A deftly camouflaged, but still very visible inner shift of levels,

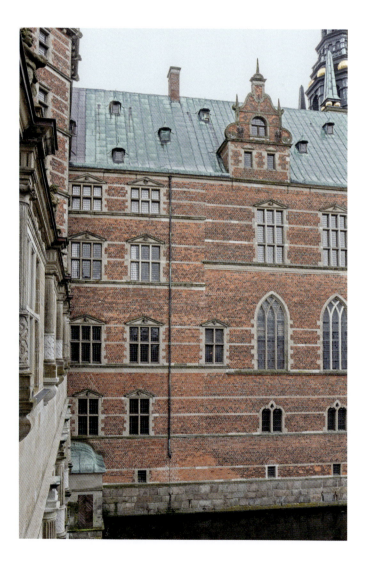

FIG. 3.3. The transition from the Chapel Wing to the Royal Wing on the western facade shows an uncoordinated change of plans during the actual building of this section (September 1606 onwards). The Chapel was suddenly given much greater height, an increase of c.1.8 metres, which emerges clearly from the visible clash between the sandstone decoration of the already finished Royal Wing to the left and the new Chapel Wing to the right (cf. fig. 3.4 and 3.11). The photograph shows the view from the Audience House's east window, across the moat and with the Privy Gallery to the left.

III · THEOBALDS, AND AFTER   33

FIG. 3.4. The unforeseen greater height of the Chapel necessitated the introduction of a staircase facilitating access from the Royal Wing to the Great Hall situated right above the Chapel. This reconstructed space, which Ferdinand Meldahl gave a new monumental centrality, illustrates the original, rather abrupt shift in level of just about 1.8 metres.

precisely where old meets new, still illustrates this new dimensioning (fig. 3.4).

Whatever the trigger for this alteration of plans, it gloriously resulted in a chapel space that combines tall Gothic formats on the exterior with a gilded, classical-style interior that on clear days is bathed in light from top to bottom. In the long line of Protestant princely chapels, beginning at the Torgau Chapel in Saxony consecrated by Luther himself, the Chapel at Frederiksborg, which was consecrated on the hundredth anniversary of the Lutheran Reformation, stands out as among the most magnificent. As for the unknown architect, the leading expert, the late Hugo Johannsen, plausibly picked out the Dresden sculptor and architect Giovanni Maria Nosseni (1544–1620) as having been somehow involved, not on the spot, but by sending drawings and proposals. Whatever the truth, we are certainly going to find unmistakable evidence of Nosseni's involvement in other parts of the project.[2]

But to return to the overriding impression of plans being revised and raised to an altogether more ambitious level, it is, to understand the second set of evidence, vital to remember that Frederiksborg was, so to speak, built backwards, beginning with the Royal Wing and the side wings, first the eastern, then the western, that were then joined (rather inelegantly) by a fairly lack-lustre brick wall and a pair of still extant, flat-roofed gateway pavilions flanking the central gateway (1609).[3] Then work started on the Forecourt (c.1608 onwards) and on the Tiltyard (1614), but looking more closely at these latter projects it becomes clear that the king and his master builders had now begun to operate on the basis of an entirely new modular with powerful overall stress on the Classical Orders, on symmetry, and on regularity. Gone now was the originally much more "Gothic" and picturesquely asymmetrical aesthetic that characterises the early phase.[4]

This reorientation was remarkably expansive. There is no sign, anymore, of this castle becoming just a taller and bulkier version of the manor house residences of the king's members of council. When logistics permitted and everyone could move into the new central wings (the court and administration needed undisturbed lodgings), all the buildings in the old Forecourt were torn down, the area flattened and expanded sideways. On this new and broader lot two almost identical side wings were erected, their facades, towers and sandstone decoration and their curving Dutch gables closely echoing those of the castle's side wings, but substantially sparser and lower and positioned so widely apart that by broadening the Forecourt they emphasise and make visible the imposing bulk of the castle itself. The Forecourt's less exuberant facade adornments and more subdued curving gables make the crescendo of this inverted architectural perspective even more impressive.

A few years later the sculptor Adriaen de Vries would deliver, from the Imperial court in Prague, the great Neptune fountain, which was installed right at the Forecourt's centre. Further to emphasise the axis of symmetry, the king's new master builder, Hans van Steenwinckel the Younger and his partner Hans Reiman, would in 1620, almost at the end of Frederiksborg's building history, tear down the originally diagonal access bridge from the south and replace it with the so-called S-bridge. This winding new bridge takes the visitor some 15 metres to the east before again turning due north, directly towards the castle's new and imposing Gateway Tower that, with its splendid spire, creates a suitably monumental entrance to the inner compound. With its steeply rising pinnacle, the tower closely echoes the gateway tower of the old Copenhagen Castle, the eponymous Blue Tower, that rose imperiously above the ancestral citadel and that still, in its third incarnation, remains one of Copenhagen's landmarks.

By this sideways move, visitors would no longer approach the castle along the diagonal route laid out and walled in between the stables built by Christian's father, an oblique approach that lets the visitor see the *point de vue* of the castle's main facade slightly at an angle. Instead, entry was now, by the introduction of the winding *figura serpentinata* of the S-bridge, redirected and orchestrated so that all access is front-on, directly along the castle's visually stunning, roughly 125 metres long north-south axis of symmetry – a re-alignment that, as has rightly been said, "brought the Baroque to Denmark" in one spectacular move.

Originally it had also been the king's intention to tear down the buildings from his father's days on the first island, an intervention that would have allowed him to have a much longer and even more stupendous route of front-on access, all the way from the City Gate onwards. But nothing came of it, be it for aesthetic or practical reasons. Perhaps the surprising change of focus created by the S-bridge was an effect deemed sufficiently stunning in separating the bland, utilitarian stables architecture of the first island from the increasing splendour of the castle's Forecourt and Inner Courtyard.[5]

What remains is therefore a very mannerist and, at the same time, baroque visual experience that suddenly and impressively shifts from the original diagonal approach to a new, head-on symmetricity. By this new access, from below the great Gateway Tower past the water cascades of the Neptune fountain and onwards to the bridge that stands symmetrically framed by the columns and by the wings of the Terrace, the sheer visual exuberance, but also the impression of visual harmony, balance and classical regularity, are consistently and memorably sustained (fig. 3.5–6).

Steenwinckel's new Terrace was an intricate part of this overall realignment. As we have seen, his predecessor had divided Forecourt from Inner Courtyard by means of a fortress-like brick wall (fig. 3.2) with a still-preserved pair of flat-roofed guardsmen's lodges in the middle. Whatever the details, such lack-lustre

division would simply no longer do. What was needed was something classical, harmonious and splendid, an architectural screen, as it were, with the sculptures and arcades laid out so as to close off the Forecourt and symmetrically frame the entrance to the Inner Courtyard. Thereby, it would ultimately prepare visitors for the even more magnificent things to come.

The tearing down of one facade and replacing it with a new was clearly neither foreseen nor planned from the beginning. Far from it. If ever there were an original, comprehensive masterplan for the whole

FIG. 3.5. Bird's-eye view of Frederiksborg which illustrates how the reorientation of the so-called S-bridge changes the originally diagonal approach through the first courtyard built under King Christian's father to the strictly linear approach along the axis of symmetry.

FIG. 3.6. Ground plan of Frederiksborg prior to the fire in 1859. From Meldahl 1887. From south to north (upwards) the three-island compound is some 275 metres long.

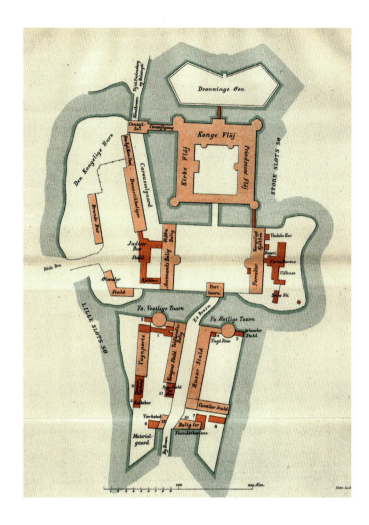

complex, everything suggests that such a plan was strongly modified, albeit in different tempos and with diverse focus, in a process first adumbrated in late 1606 and then, to an increasing degree, implemented. This reorientation would ultimately and sensationally culminate in the complete refashioning of the facade of the Royal Wing, which at the very end of the building process came into critical focus, its original layout of early 1606 now being completely remodelled. But more on this in the following chapters (ch. IV–VI).

The question to be examined here is what triggered

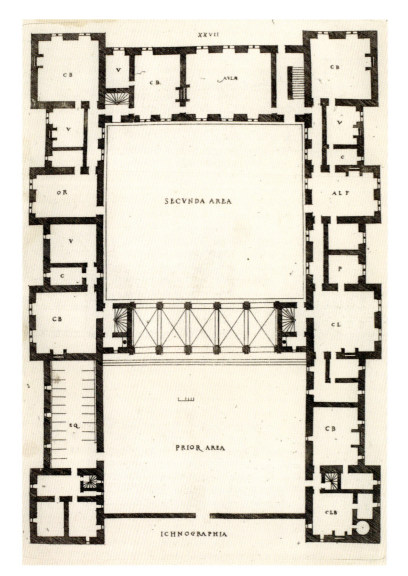

FIG. 3.7. Ground plan from Jacques Androuet du Cerceau, *De architectura*, Paris 1559, tab. xxvii.

these changes? That the king welcomed and, in part, also instigated them is, as we shall see, clear. But what inspired them?

It is commonly agreed that the inspiration for the solution in the form of the one-storey Terrace with its richly adorned facade and its balustraded flat roof ultimately hails from France. So does the Italianate loggia at its rear (fig. 3.16). Whether directly or otherwise, the model for creating this sequence of a symmetrically balanced "forecourt" (*prior area*) that gives access through a lower gateway wing to a more richly decorated and monumental "inner courtyard" (*secunda area*) is to be found in the *Livre d'architecture* (fig. 3.7) by the renowned French architect Jacques Androuet du Cerceau (1510–c.1580). The engravings of this and du Cerceau's later works had an immense influence on the early seventeenth-century architecture of the Netherlands and beyond.[6]

There is no evidence that Steenwinckel or any of the king's other master builders ever visited France. To be sure, Steenwinckel must have trained in the Netherlands and doubtless knew du Cerceau's books,[7] but it is one thing to see a plan on a page, another to actually experience how impressive it is to approach a residence through such a well-ordered sequence of courtyards, each more lavish than the last. Add to this that Steenwinckel only became involved in the building of the castle in 1614. By then the new emphasis on symmetry and axiality had long since manifested itself.

So, for a "prime mover" we must look elsewhere. Various names such as that of Steenwinckel the Elder, who died in 1601, have been put forward; while plausible, they are for lack of evidence not entirely convincing. However, in this context, it has commonly gone unnoticed that King Christian had in fact himself visited such a palatial, French-style building complex with just such a stately succession of courtyards; this was in 1606 when he and his brother-in-law, King James I, were, for four days, from 24 to 28 July, the guests of the latter's Secretary of State, Robert Cecil, the Earl of Salisbury, at his already then legendary residence at Theobalds.

We owe the suggestion of a possible link to Theobalds to the Danish Christian IV expert Meir Stein, who, however, did not pursue the matter in any detail.[8] This is perhaps the reason why his idea has never caught on, let alone even been discussed. As will become apparent, it is, however, worth the while to follow the lead and take a hard look at the evidence revealing what King Christian would have seen in July 1606 and how this experience might have affected the subsequent development of Frederiksborg.

Located some twelve miles north of London, the magnificent Theobalds was described in a contemporary travel account of which King Christian owned a copy as "one of the most beautiful Houses in England." Indeed, it was one of the largest residences ever to be built there. In the words of the eminent English art historian John Summerson, its line of courtyards was "deployed in expansive symmetry across a quarter-mile axis extending to the London road."[9] By this arrangement Theobalds' main house was approached through two closely aligned and increasingly splendid courtyards that finally reached the principal house with the so-called Fountain Court, from which there was access to the royal apartments, originally of Queen Elizabeth, now of King James. Along this approach and across a distance of some 400 metres, one could see, "when the gates are open", the "figure of Cupid and Venus" on the fountain in the Fountain Court. "The like walke", it was said at the time, "for lengthe, pleasantness and Delight is rare to be seene in England."[10]

Of this iconic residence almost nothing remains. A symbol of Stuart "tyranny", it was completely levelled under Cromwell. However, in 1959 John Summerson brilliantly reassembled a set of plans of the Cecils' marvel or, as Summerson termed it, "prodigy house",

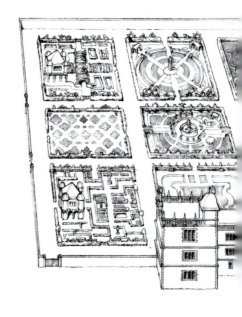

FIG. 3.8. Conjectural reconstruction of the exterior of Theobalds, viewed from the south-east, and showing the principal courtyards, projecting gallery range, Base Court and some of the gardens.
Allan Adams © Historic England. Reproduced with generous permission by Dr Emily Cole and her colleagues at Historic England.

42 · III · THEOBALDS, AND AFTER

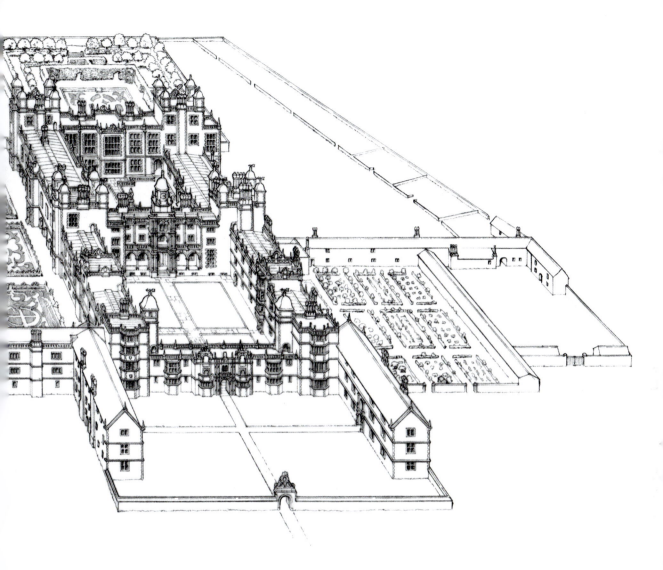

roughly as it presented itself during the visit of King Christian.[11] Through archaeology and painstaking study of descriptions, ground plans and elevations, this pioneering work has since then been supplemented and enriched, so that a detailed and reliable, but, of course conjectural, image now has emerged (fig. 3.8).

If we compare a typical du Cerceau layout with that of Theobalds and Frederiksborg, the similarities are striking (fig. 3.6–8). All three have a *prior* and a *secunda area* of great regularity around an axis of symmetry.

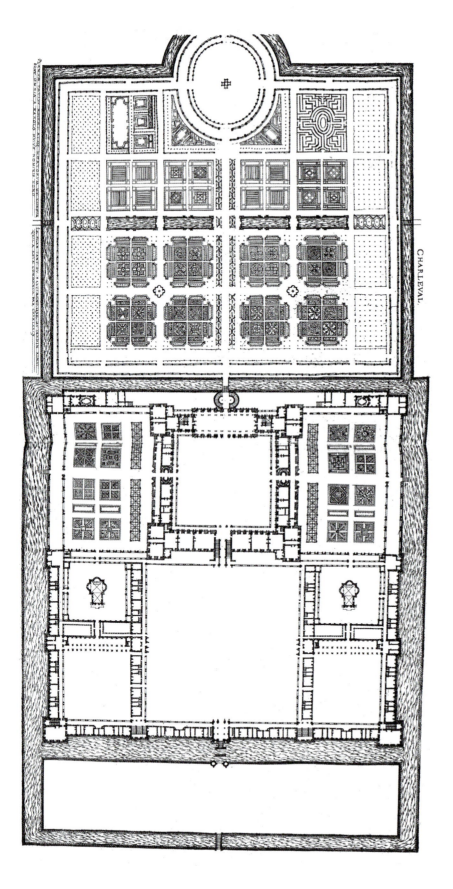

FIG. 3.9. Ground plan of the never completed *Charleval* (1570). From Jacques Androuet du Cerceau, "Charleval" in *Les plus excellents Bastiments de France*, vol. II, Paris 1579.

Unusually, Theobalds then has a third and final courtyard (a departure that has to do with the fact that the Cecil residence doubled as a royal residence). But as in du Cerceau and at Frederiksborg it is the link between the *prior* and *secunda area* that matters. Two aspects seem notable. While, in the ground plan commonly quoted to illustrate similarities (fig. 3.7), du Cerceau has a Forecourt and Inner Courtyard of identical width, the dimensions of one duplicating the other, Theobalds and Frederiksborg both opt for forecourts of sufficient extra width to ensure that the *whole* central building corpus with the highly ornate oriels and, at Frederiksborg, curving gables of the side wings would be on panoramic display. This was in fact a solution not unknown to du Cerceau, who has a similar wide-screen forecourt in the designs for King Charles IX of France's vast (and never completed) palace of Charleval (fig. 3.9).[12] Whatever the inspiration it is notable, however, that Theobalds and Frederiksborg share this aspect in their overall ground plan.

What further seems notable is that, at the intersection of these two courtyards, Frederiksborg and Theobalds closely follow du Cerceau in having a lower so-called terrace, two-storey at Theobalds and one-storey at Frederiksborg, a flat-roofed and balustraded gateway building that in the French manner separates as well as connects the courtyards.

As in du Cerceau, moreover, the *en terrace* gateways of the two residences themselves had loggias at the rear – but what is crucial is that at both edifices in question the rear-side loggias were answered, at the opposite side of the *secunda area*, by an even more impressive two-storey loggia[13] or "stone gallery"[14] (thus a British account of Theobalds) that in *both* cases had been delivered by sculptors in the Netherlands.[15] In the circle around Cornelis Floris (1514–75) in Antwerp, the manufacture of such ready-made loggias for far off clients became part of what sculptors in the Low Countries were known to offer.[16] Both the sandstone galleries in question, Lord Cecil's from Antwerp, King Christian's from Amsterdam, were richly ornamented architectural screens of such dimensions that, in colour and surface, they not only set off the principal facade clearly from the red-brick masonry of the surrounding facades, but their gilded top sections would in either case rise so high that they were visible from the Forecourt. Both, moreover, shielded a richly decorated first-floor walkway that connected the compound's side wings across the main facade.[17] To top off this series of similarities it should finally be noted that like Theobalds' royal Fountain Court, the Inner Courtyard of Frederiksborg was adorned with a – yes, your guess is correct! – *Venus & Cupid* fountain (fig. 3.10).

These similarities, in the disposition of *prior* and *secunda area*, in the use of terraced gateways and of loggias of extravagant, increasing monumentality (both the latter from the Netherlands at that), in cross-facade walkways and finally in the deployment of centrally displayed *Venus & Cupid* fountains, seem too numerous and too specific to be merely coincidental. Of course, there is no doubt that du Cerceau was of basic, common importance for the two projects, but there is so much at Frederiksborg that recalls Theobalds in telling detail that the overriding, specific importance of King Christian's visit in 1606 for his own project seems to go far beyond reasonable doubt.

Even more so because King Christian is known to have had rich opportunity during his stay to take detailed note of it all (fig. 3.8). On his arrival, he was first greeted, with much ceremony and at great length, at

FIG. 3.10. Jørgen Wulff, fountain in bronze with *Venus & Cupid*, 1619–20. Originally placed in the Inner Courtyard of Frederiksborg, opposite the Chapel Wing. Looted by the Swedish army in 1659, the original is now to be found in the park of the royal palace of Drottningholm outside Stockholm. The version now at Frederiksborg is a cast. The basin in the shape of a mussel alludes to the seaborne origins of Venus. The sandstone frame with the relief of a nymph abducted by yet another sea-god (cf. fig. 5.7–8) is by Hans van Steenwinckel (1620).

the gate to the Base Court, where a shower of "welcome(s)" written in golden letters on leaves made of silk were dropped from the trees framing the access route; ceremonies were then resumed, reaching their culmination when the kings passed through the entrance to the Middle Court and paused before its imposing "stone Gallery", where from the top of the flat-roofed gateway or, perhaps, from the gallery itself they would hear more such welcomes written by Ben Jonson and staged by Inigo Jones. The stone gallery of Theobalds was the work of the Flemish sculptor Hendrik van Paesschen and shipped from Flanders across

III · THEOBALDS, AND AFTER   47

to England in 1569–70. Van Paesschen had supplied similar stone work from Flanders for Queen Elizabeth's Royal Exchange in London.

Like the other witnesses, an anonymous Danish diarist accompanying the king leaves the location of these histrionics uncertain, merely describing how three boys, handsomely dressed, "were standing in niches beautifully decked out with cloth", when greeting the monarchs. But whatever the location, the architecture was clearly no mute and irrelevant setting for this eagerly followed royal visit, the first in England for more than eighty years.[18] Visibly and audibly, the hugely costly ceremonies surrounding this sensational visit were framed by and embedded in Theobalds' whole architectural layout.[19]

During the following days at Theobalds there was clearly much drinking and carousing, which has come to dominate modern accounts, to obscuring effect. The fact that the primary witness of this drunkenness and also vomiting, a disaffected courtier and godson of the late queen named John Harington, had an axe to grind with the Stuart court and, *eo ipso*, also with its royal in-law, should make us wary of taking his allegations completely at face value. In his account of the theatricals[20] at Theobalds there are in fact aspects, as the Shakespeare scholar James Shapiro has recently shown, that seem exaggerated.[21] This is not to say that festivities were teetotal.[22] As immortalised by Shakespeare, the king of Denmark's festive approach to alcohol was indeed proverbially familiar:

> And let the kettle to the trumpet speak,
> the trumpets to the cannoneer without,
> the cannons to the heavens, the heavens to earth:
> "Now the King drinks…" (*Hamlet*, Act v, sc. ii)

However, King Christian's keen and trained eye for architecture is also well documented. In London, he had looked attentively at the main sights – the Tower, the Royal Exchange, St Paul's and Westminster. At the Exchange, it was noted how he walked through both the upper and lower loggias, diligently observing everything, and then "sate downe upon the long bench, at the East side, and behelde the manner of the building"[23] (he would later build his own two-storey Exchange in Copenhagen, one of the great monuments of his reign). In Westminster Abbey, where his host had ordered the funerary images of a series of royal predecessors including Queen Elizabeth to be splendidly decked out with their royal robes and put on display in Henry the Seventh's Chapel,[24] it seems suggestive that (as it is reported) "King Christianus ... tooke most notice of St. Edward's shrine, and therewithall admired the whole architecture and fabrication."[25] The sight of the Abbey's soaring Gothic style may well have influenced the king's sudden decision to make his own Castle Chapel dramatically higher than originally planned (fig. 3.3–4). The visit goes far in explaining the unparalleled, in Denmark, and very "Tudoresque" quality of its richly gilded, Gothic vaulting; the similarity to the vaulting of Windsor's St George's Chapel (where Christian became a Knight of the Garter) also seems suggestive (3.11).[26] In any case, it was noted that on his visits to Greenwich, Whitehall, Richmond, Hampton Court and Windsor, "the King of Denmarke was very much delighted, with the gallantnesse of these Royall Pallaces of his Maiestie; as did appear by his earnest noting of them."[27] Surely, an enthusiastic builder such as King Christian would on such occasions have used his eyes well. Years earlier, in 1597, his improvised *incognito* visit to Dresden was "solely" motivated by his

FIG. 3.11. The Frederiksborg Castle Chapel.

FIG. 3.12. The remnants of the Munitions Hall of the *Zeughaus* in Dresden, later incorporated into the *Albertinum* art museum, where it survived the apocalyptic Second World War bombardment. The hall, which King Christian travelled to see in 1597, is 74 metres long, with nine Tuscan columns along its central axis. Photo from 2010, just prior to the reopening of the restored *Albertinum*.

FIG. 3.13. The Munitions Hall in King Christian's *Tøjhus* in Copenhagen. The arched layout, here with sixteen central pillars, is very similar to what he had seen in Dresden, but in Copenhagen the Hall is 164 metres long. This was as much about display as about storage. The Hall, which showed the military might of Denmark, was in the seventeenth century a sightseer's must.

wish to "inspect" (*besee*) the Elector's new *Zeughaus*, which, he told his companions, compared unfavourably to what he himself was planning for Copenhagen, where his own, much grander, but, in significant respects, similar, Arsenal was completed between 1598 and 1604 (figs. 3.12–13).[28]

With his own new residence well under way, seeing and hearing how the Cecils had put the ideas of du Cerceau to such impressive use – not just at Theobalds, but, as has recently been demonstrated, also at their palatial city residence in the Strand in London[29] – is bound to have left its mark. The Cecils, first father, then son, had since the earliest years of the great Queen Bess been key political figures in Protestant Europe, a rank so clearly reflected in the magnificence of their palace that King James made them cede it[30] to himself and Queen Anne[31] less than a year after her brother's visit – a transfer that suggestively echoes the way Frederiksborg had been ceded by a member of the Danish nobility to the king's father. Whether or not this precedent influenced King James' decision, Theobalds was, from then onwards, to be his preferred residence. When King Christian returned from England and plans for the Frederiksborg Forecourt were being finalised, he had, in short, not only read and heard, but also actually experienced how a residence fit for a modern monarch should be laid out, to the most splendid effect. And as was well known, the king knew how to communicate with his master builders, "for their information sometimes himself giving them a draft and outline, done in his own hand" (thus the bishop, in his funeral *laudatio*).[32]

Other factors, not on record, may well have been at work, but it is hardly coincidental that it was after the visit to Theobalds that the above-mentioned aesthetic

FIG. 3.14. The south facade of the Terrace at Frederiksborg with Steenwinckel's six mythological pairs. They are framed by twelve arches, each statue standing in an ornate sandstone niche (two of the original statues have later been replaced).

realignment in the dimension and construction of Frederiksborg started to manifest itself. What comes to the fore now and in the years leading up to 1622 is a recurrent overall tendency for the symmetry axis of the whole complex to be increasingly emphasised (fig. 3.14). As we shall see, the facade of the Terrace was in fact deliberately laid out not just to round off the Forecourt but also to prepare the visitor for the display in the Inner Courtyard, planned, but still not installed, with which the visual programme was now intended to culminate.

Steenwinckel gave the Terrace facade this heralding character by introducing a set of avowedly classical architectural motifs such as Tuscan columns, arches and mannerist quasi-*aedicula* crowned by pediments, each to shelter a statue of gods or heroes from Gre-

FIG. 3.15. The architect and his royal patron? Painting ascribed to Karel van Mander, c.1640, oil on canvas, 63 × 80. The Royal Danish Collection, Rosenborg. The engineer or architect portrayed in the company of the king and with Rosenborg in the background has by some been identified as a posthumous portrait of Steenwinckel. Of Dutch origin Hans van Steenwinckel the Younger (1587–1639) followed his father in working as sculptor and architect. In 1619 he rose to be the king's chief architect with numerous tasks at Frederiksborg and Roskilde as well as in Copenhagen (the Royal Exchange, the Round Tower and the Trinity Church). Denmark's leading architect during an unusually productive reign, his *oeuvre* has had a lasting impact.

co-Roman antiquity, which now joined the figures of the Neptune fountain in greeting the visitor (fig. 3.15). Steenwinckel was no doubt constrained to preserve as much as possible not only of his predecessor's cubic sentry posts framing the gateway, but also of the splendid coat of arms above it. This still displays the year 1609, but the rest is, by and large, from ten years later. For the new sections Steenwinckel chose to adopt a loggia format that on the side facing the Forecourt is pure external facade, its arcades added on to the walls linking the castle's side wings. At the rear, however, Steenwinckel created a real, classical loggia, among the earliest of its kind to be preserved in Scandinavia (fig. 3.16).[33]

On the outer facade, twelve arches frame statues that were once gilded and that were positioned, just like the insignia of the king and queen, in pairs, three on each side of the portal.[34] The profuse use of gilding

FIG. 3.16. Steenwinckel's loggia with two times five arcades on the side of the Terrace facing the Inner Courtyard. The similarities with de Keyser's Exchange in Amsterdam (1608–11), which Steenwinckel had probably seen, as well as with London's Royal Exchange (1566–67), which King Christian visited and admired in 1606, are obvious.

on the facades of Frederiksborg is yet another feature with parallels in England: at his sister's palace of Nonsuch, which King Christian briefly visited on 8 August 1606, the facades were packed with gilded stuccos, an aspect certainly impressing a Danish courtier in the king's entourage.[35] But whatever the inspiration for this aspect, the statues at Frederiksborg were distributed according to a hierarchical, male/female and symmetrical principle, which, like the number twelve, is once again a feature that is repeated in the Inner Courtyard. These statues have of course all lost their original gilding and they have, to a considerable degree, either been recut or replaced during the eighteenth and nineteenth centuries.

Although badly preserved, they are, however, still recognisable: the gateway itself is flanked by the most eminent of the gods – to the west below the king's badge *Jupiter & Juno*, to the east below that of the queen *Neptune & Amphitrite*. Then follow *Venus & Mars* (west) and to the east *Hercules & Minerva* (the latter a replacement for an original *Omphale*). As personifications of strength and beauty – and of female power over men – both couples figure prominently in Renaissance

FIG. 3.17. Hendrick van Balen, *Atalanta & Hippomenes*, c. 1619, oil on canvas, 58.4 × 21.3. Rijksmuseum, Amsterdam.

art; in the decoration of Frederiksborg they are also on constant display.

To the west, at the end of the row, one finds *Atalanta & Hippomenes*, which is rather surprising.[36] But in their capacity as the stars of antiquity's and the Renaissance's most famous mythological race they are aptly positioned close to where the facade borders on the Tiltyard; furthermore, it was Venus, here positioned right next to *Hippomenes*, who gave him the golden apples that secured his victory in the race. *Hippomenes*

FIG. 3.18. Heinrich Hansen, *The Great Hall at Frederiksborg in the days of Christian IV*, c.1858–64, oil on canvas, 89 × 121.7. Cheltenham Art Gallery & Museum. The reconstruction is based upon the painter's detailed pre-fire studies of the tapestries, ceiling and the monumental Apollo fireplace in dark marble and with figures and ornaments in silver. The tapestry in the background shows the coronation procession of Christian IV. A lithograph after this painting was published in a popular series of *tableaux* edited in 1872.

would no doubt have been depicted running, in one hand holding the golden apples in a net, while with the other throwing a tempting apple backwards in the direction of *Atalanta*, whose attention is captured, as she turns towards her competitor – a fine symbol of the kind of festive competition that was seen unfolding on the neighbouring Tiltyard (cf. ch. VII). *Hippo*menes' horse-evoking name (*hippos* is Greek for "horse") would only have made this association clearer (fig. 3.17).

Similarly, with the couple standing at the end of the eastward row, *Phoebus & Luna*, also known as *Apollo & Diana*: At a court where the pleasure of music and hunting was highly rated the goddess of hunting and the god of the arts are natural components in the imagery. In Frederiksborg's Great Hall the Apollo fireplace (fig. 3.18) was one of the pre-eminent sights; so was the chandelier, named after the huntress Diana. Indeed, hunting remained a constant in the iconography – and in the *raison d'être* – of the castle. In the forests to its north, King Christian's successors would during the seventh and eighteenth centuries lay out a vast *par force* hunting area that in its uniquely well-preserved deployment of baroque landscaping principles represents an impressive geography of centralised power. Now a much visited wild-life zone, it has just recently been declared a UNESCO World Heritage Monument.[37]

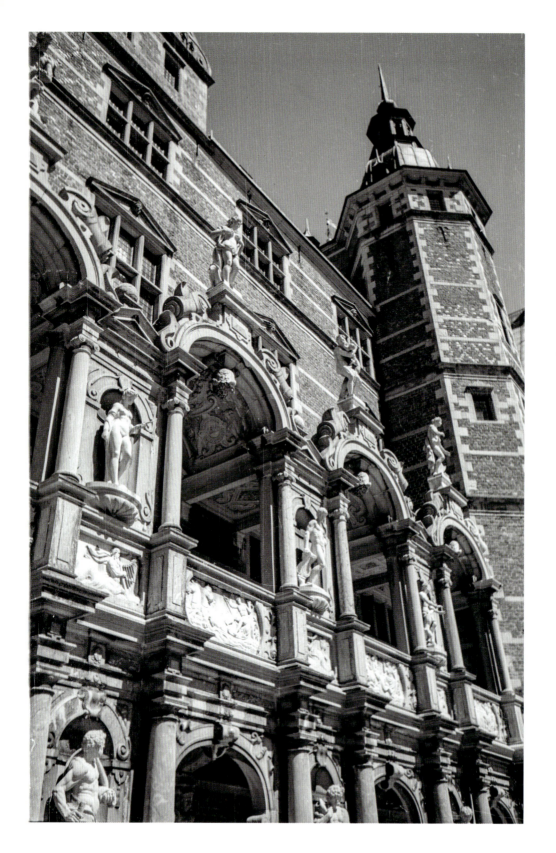

FIG. 4.1. The Gallery at Frederiksborg. Photo by Keld Helmer-Petersen from 1943. The Royal Danish Library.

IV

The Marble Gallery

PASSING FROM THE OUTER TO THE INNER Courtyard the visitor comes face to face with the culmination of this series of richly decorated sculptural and architectural *tableaux*. With its seven two-storey bays crowned by a line of seven freestanding sculptures standing high upon the top arches, the castle's so-called Marble (in fact sandstone) Gallery repeats and expands the decorative scheme of the Terrace, but now to the height of almost three storeys (1619–21). On entering the Inner Courtyard, this opulent *frons scaenae* immediately commands full attention. The *Venus & Cupid* Fountain to the right (fig. 3.10) and the imposing tower of the Chapel Wing to the left provide a degree of visual counterpoint. Still, the Marble Gallery effectively steals the show (fig. 4.2).

Metaphors from the world of the stage are at this point apt, because the Marble Gallery is no original component of the architecture. In fact it is in a sense a set piece introduced to mask a fundamental asymmetry that must soon have felt awkward.[1] As it was originally conceived (fig. 4.3), the central section of the Royal Wing's principal facade completely lacked the imposing monumentality that by 1620 was becoming *de rigueur* throughout cultured Europe.[2] Instead of a centrally placed main entrance of proportions, style and adornment that was fully in keeping with royal status (fig. 4.4), this principal facade was originally laid out in time-honoured medieval fashion with stair turrets

FIG. 4.2. Frederiksborg. The Inner Courtyard with the Gallery. The courtyard measures c. 40 × 40 metres.

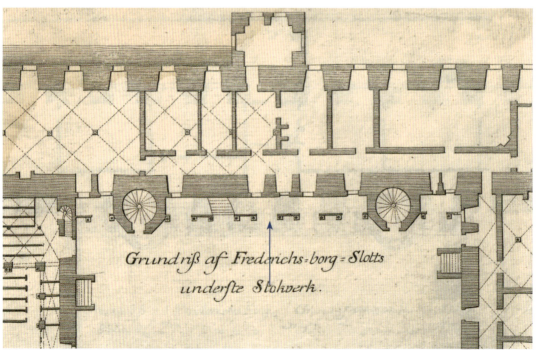

64 &ep; IV · THE MARBLE GALLERY

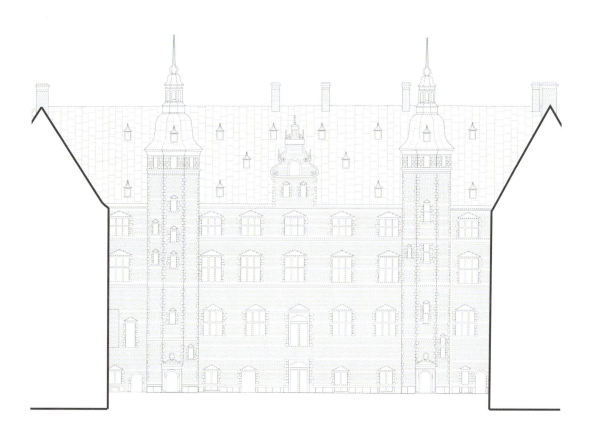

FIG. 4.3. Frederiksborg. The ground plan and facade of the Royal Wing facing the Inner Courtyard as it originally appeared. Note the "medieval" irregularity in the positioning of the windows and ground-floor gateways on the original brick facade of 1606. The central symmetry axis (indicated by the inserted arrow) is met by a bit of wall and an off-centre window, not an entrance (but Meldahl changed this: fig. 4.4). The Gallery and the first-floor windows are unaligned (also changed by Meldahl: fig. 4.4). The crowning gable is 1.25 metres off centre. Thurah 1749, pl. vi and x.

FIG. 4.4. Frederiksborg. The 1606 facade as restored by Meldahl. Digital reconstruction by Kirsten Marie Kragelund. To create an illusion of an originally non-existing symmetry, Meldahl inserted an imposing, heavily framed gateway in the ground-floor centre. The *piano nobile* window directly above this new gateway was also completely refashioned (cf. fig. 4.14) and is, in contrast to the original, now crowned by a heavily ornate, curved pediment. Most of the first-floor windows were repositioned, so that they now are in alignment with the Gallery. The result of these interventions is that the building's roots in an at first far less regular aesthetic are made less obvious. This hardly fulfils Meldahl's declared aim to restore the building as "it had been in the days of Christian IV": cf. fig. 7.13 and ch. IV, n. 16.

IV · THE MARBLE GALLERY 65

in the corners of the courtyard, the turret to the west giving access to the king's apartments, the one to the east to the queen's; as tradition prescribed – and as it could still be seen, for instance in the palaces of Copenhagen and Berlin – these towers were connected by a wooden balcony, a so-called "svalegang".[3] In the eyes of contemporaries, especially from abroad, this disposition would have left the central section of the principal facade oddly, not to say clumsily, unremarkable, the very asymmetrical position of the ground-floor windows and entrances completely unaligned with the more regular first-, second- and third-floor windows. Even the crowning triangular gable (originally gilded, at that) is, on closer inspection, dizzyingly off-centre.

Tellingly, this facade was in its irregularity not unlike that built by his father Frederik II at Kronborg some twenty years earlier (fig. 4.5) – but this was clearly no longer a style King Christian wanted to imitate.

In view of the strongly emphasised overall symmetry of the route of access, of the facades and of the Forecourt, such irregularity, which Steenwinckel had inherited from his predecessor, is bound to have come across as an anti-climax.

More than anything, it is this clash of aesthetic principles that shows how Theobalds must have been a revelation for King Christian. If there from the very beginning had been a du Cerceau-inspired masterplan for Frederiksborg, with a 120 meters symmetry-axis from the Gateway all the way up to the façade, it seems unthinkable that one would have accepted a *point de vue* facade of such irregularity.

With the visit to Theobalds in mind it is a fair guess that Steenwinckel and the king were in complete agreement as to the necessity of remedying this situation. A plan was devised to mask the asymmetry with

FIG. 4.5. The Royal Wing of Frederik II's Kronborg Castle at Elsinore with the Chapel below and the Great Hall above. 1580s. The facade is laid out in the traditional manner, from the inside out, not from the outside in. Thurah 1749, pl. xxix.

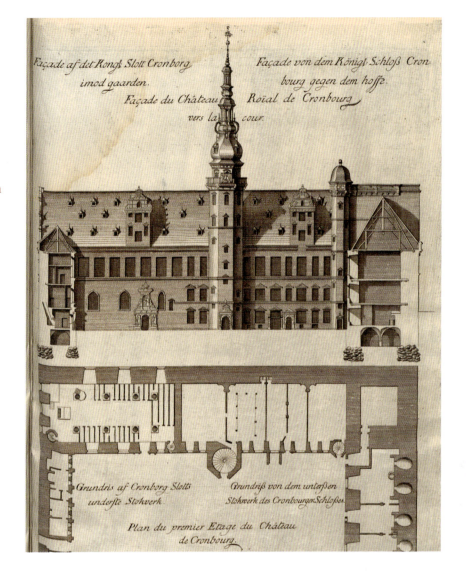

a marble gallery that would provide what was needed. The inspiration for this intervention has often been sought in France, but again Theobalds offers an equally or even more weighty parallel, namely the "stone Gallery" that the Cecils had imported from Flanders and set up on the palace's principal facade facing the Middle Court (fig. 3.8). The emphatic shift in material, surface and colour, from dominantly red-brick to the no doubt richly ornamented, whitish sandstone gallery

with a gilded coat of arms on its top – all this would have shown King Christian how the red-brick facade of his own Royal Wing back home could be given the proper crowning *extra*.

For his choice of an open stone gallery with classical arches there are other weighty parallels to consider.[4] Even if the dimensions are different it seems relevant to point to the three-storey loggia (fig. 5.1) on the south facade of the residence of the king's grandfather, the Duke of Mecklenburg, in Güstrow (where he stayed as a child and returned as a youth) and above all to the loggia in the Great Courtyard in the Electors' Residence in Dresden. Frequent intermarriage between the Protestant courts of Mecklenburg, Saxony and Denmark ensured a lively cultural dialogue, Mecklenburg and Saxony often showing the Danish

FIG. 4.6. The Gallery in the Great *Schlosshof* in the Residence in Dresden. The ongoing reconstruction aims at showing the facades and Gallery of the *Schlosshof* as they would have looked during the reign of the Protestant Elector Moritz, when this was the most *avant-garde* residence in the Protestant North.

68 · IV · THE MARBLE GALLERY

in-laws what was hot in European fashion.⁵ In their residence in Dresden, which King Christian visited in 1597, access to the upper storeys was likewise through corner stair turrets, but in order to give the central section of the palace's north wing suitable emphasis, the elector Moritz (1521–53) added an imposing, richly frescoed, four-storeyed gallery, Tuscan below, then Ionic, Corinthian and, finally, Composite. This gallery is defiantly Protestant in its iconography, being a clear polemical echo of the very similar, four-storey gallery of the Papal Palace in the Vatican.⁶ In practical terms, however, it frames no central entrance, but gives the facade a unifying centre while at the same time serving as a monumental eye-catcher below the towering *Hausmannsturm* (fig. 4.6).

In Denmark, s similar solution was adopted. Memories of Dresden and, above all, Theobalds may at this point be said to have merged. The original, old-fashioned wooden gallery that from 1606 had linke the facade's stair turrets was now replaced by a gallery designed by Steenwinckel. Of course, this solution could not completely hide the fact that the doorways and windows of the original ground and first floor were in sometimes jarring unalignment with the Gallery's arches; moreover, the solution went no deeper than the facade: by entering one of the facade's central, or rather, off-centre, gateways one would have been standing either in the kitchen area or in a guardsmen's sentry box with only indirect access to the upper storeys. But then all visitors of rank would have entered the castle by using the stair turrets going directly up to the second, third and fourth storeys.

Seventeenth-century visitors from abroad would comment negatively on this discrepancy between splendid exterior and the lack of a correspondingly monumental inner staircase.[7] Indeed, this was a drawback that was never remedied.[8] Still, the new plans for the facade have the obvious aesthetic merit of creating an *illusion* of regularity, thereby bringing the whole of the Theobalds- and the du Cerceau-inspired route of access to a visually satisfying and, indeed, triumphant conclusion.

Work started in or around 1619, when Steenwinckel contacted the renowned architect Hendrick de Keyser in Amsterdam, asking him to deliver columns and mouldings, statues and reliefs for the planned gallery. During Steenwinckel's years of apprentice, de Keyser had probably been his mentor. By 1619, de Keyser had just embarked on the project of providing the partly burnt-out town hall at Delft with a new, richly ornamented facade, a work that with its use of sandstone, coloured marble and gilded detail has been characterised as a veritable "showpiece of de Keyser's 'modern' variation on the Classical Orders." King Christian ordered something similar for his own residence, a fine example of the way Dutch civic architecture in this period set standards that were followed throughout much of Northern Europe. Between 1619 and 1622 there are reports showing how sandstone was shipped duty free from the Baltic all the way to Amsterdam and how de Keyser's "trusted foreman" Gerrit Lambertsen at some point transferred his workshop to Elsinore, where the project was to be completed.[9] As was the case with the Cecils at Theobalds, King Christian would only be content with the best.

In its earliest known design, one hears only of reliefs and statues of the seven planet-gods. But plans evolved and the Gallery's niches that had probably initially been intended to stand unadorned were eventually also given a series of statues echoing – and sometimes

FIG. 4.7. *Julius Caesar*. The first in a series of the twelve Suetonian Caesars, from Caesar himself to Domitian that were put up in the pediments of the windows of the Eastern Wing of Frederiksborg's ground-floor and *piano nobile* windows. The sandstone has traces of colouring. According to Berg's description from 1646, gilding was also used, probably on the diadems. From the early renaissance onwards, Suetonius' twelve biographies from ca. 120 AD gave rise to a much-used decorative scheme that, irrespective of the qualities of the single emperor, gave the ensemble canonical status.

actually duplicating – those of the Terrace, the overall aim no doubt being that this stunning, even overwhelming display should dazzle visitors with a wealth of profane sculpture hitherto unseen in Scandinavia.

In the pediments over the windows the castle was already adorned with series of richly coloured portraits of Roman emperors as well as legendary and historical kings of Denmark. While the original position of the Danish monarchs is hard to decipher,[10] Berg is explicit about the "Roman Emperors", here taken to be the twelve Roman Caesars known from Suetonius' canonical biographies, originally adorning the courtyard facade of the eastern wing. With *Julius Caesar* leading off (fig. 4.7), eight of these coloured and, in those days, also gilded portraits still survive – but not, be it noted, in their original position. After the fire in 1859, it seems that the chief restorer Ferdinand Meldahl (fig. 4.13) transferred most of them to the principal facade. Whatever the date of the transfer, each of these Cae-

IV · THE MARBLE GALLERY 71

FIG. 4.8. Lauritz Albert Winstrup, reconstruction of the original colour scheme of the upper section of the Royal Wing's central facade, August 1835, paper and watercolour, 21.4 × 28.4. Danish National Art Library.

sars is originally marked with an explanatory number and name (the numbers probably meant to ensure that the masons got it right).[11] Traces of colouring (red for faces, blue and green for backgrounds) could still be seen clearly around 1910; even today, such traces show how colourful the original facades (fig. 4.8) were, not just on the ground level, but also on the *piano nobile*, where the series would have continued (as was typical in such decorations). However, only three portraits of the second half of the series seem to have survived

FIG. 4.9. The entrance to the Castle Chapel. Above the arch the figures of the legendary first Christian king of Denmark and his son and successor frame a richly decorated cartouche with the coat of arms of Christian IV at its centre. The ensemble illustrates the continuity of Danish royal piety.

the fire. The first is *Galba*, the second *Vitellius* and the third *Domitian*.

On the ground floor of the royal facade, where he without further acknowledgement chose to redeploy this decoration, Meldahl re-used *Galba* as a replacement for a lost *Tiberius*, whereas *Vitellius* is the only one still to be found on the eastern facade, but hardly *in situ*. So, the present display is a confused *bricolage*, giving no indication at all as to original provenance and context. In Denmark and, probably, Scandinavia, this only partly

IV · THE MARBLE GALLERY   73

preserved series seems to be the earliest monumental deployment of the "Twelve Caesars".¹²

Portraits of legendary and former Danish kings such as King Dan, Ragnar Lodbrog, Gorm III and Oluf III are also on record; and an unknown number are also preserved, be it *in situ* or elsewhere. Here, future investigations must unravel whether they, like the Caesars, were originally distributed according to a specific, identifiable pattern. In one such case, the pattern is clear: above the entrance to the Castle Chapel,¹³ statues of the first Christian kings of Denmark stress royal continuity in praising the Lord (fig. 4.9). "Piety Gives Strength to my Realms" (RFP or REGNA FIRMAT PIETAS) as the king's oft-repeated motto declared. King

FIG. 4.10. King Christian among his ancient peers. On the western facade of Rosenborg Castle a portrait in lead by an unknown artist was put up in this location in c.1860; here it shares company with a group of portraits of ancient worthies brought to Denmark in 1709 by King Frederik IV. The Royal Danish Collection, Rosenborg.

FIG. 4.11. King Dan, the first king of Denmark. According to legend he ruled 2898 years after the creation of the world, 1073 years before the birth of Christ. From *Chronica, das ist, Beschreibung aller Könige in Dennemarcken von dem ersten Könige Dan … bisz auff Christianum den Vierdten …*, Magdeburgk, bey Johan Francken, 1597. Francken's book reproduces portraits and verse narratives copied from the Kronborg tapestries (cf. fig. 2.4).

Christian was also elsewhere portrayed as in league with such eminent rulers as the Roman emperors (fig. 4.10). And the antiquity of his kingdom was much emphasised. As tapestries[14] (fig. 1.4) and pamphlets declared, this was the one hundred and first Danish monarch since the legendary King Dan (fig. 4.11). In addition to all this, two ensembles of thirteen reliefs and nineteen statues with figures from Greco-Roman mythology now introduced a new dimension and new narratives to the whole display. These new sculptures were, as we shall see, all positioned according to an in-

IV · THE MARBLE GALLERY   75

FIG. 4.12. Ferdinand Richardt, *The Fire at Frederiksborg in 1859*, 1859, oil on canvas, 72 × 110. The Museum of National History at Frederiksborg.

tricate and carefully laid out plan in close conjunction with the decoration by Adriaen de Vries and Steenwinckel of the Forecourt as well as with the architecture that now, as an afterthought, was being put in place.

However, due to nineteenth-century restoration a modern visitor will be unable to find any trace of such a plan and cohesion. To understand what was originally on display, a brief historical excursus is therefore necessary. The fire in 1859 (fig. 4.12) necessitated an almost complete reconstruction of the Gallery and its sculptures. With respect to the architecture, Meldahl (fig. 4.13) was reasonably faithful (but he did not live up to the original's standards of multi-colour black, red and white stone material).[15] As for sculpture, how-

FIG. 4.13. Ferdinand Meldahl (1827–1908). Painting by P.S. Krøyer, 1882, oil on canvas, 190 × 113.5. The National Gallery of Denmark.
The full-figure format adopted is indicative of the ambitions and successes of one of the period's leading Danish architects. His opulent and richly varied historicism proved hugely attractive to government officials and nobility as well as to the new upward-moving bourgeoisie. As a teacher and administrator, he dominated the Royal Academy's schools of architecture for decades. As a restorer, he was involved in most of the period's major projects, the rebuilding of Frederiksborg (1865–93) being the most prestigious.

ever, it was perhaps economy that constrained him to populate his restored Gallery with metal casts of the thirteen reliefs and the fourteen more or less fully preserved and sometimes heavily restored pre-fire statues. The casts were in zinc imitating sandstone. The procedure had its merits, since it would preserve a vestige of authenticity, but oddly the restorer aiming

IV · THE MARBLE GALLERY   77

FIG. 4.14. Ferdinand Meldahl, reconstruction drawing of the Marble Gallery. Signed and dated 12 May 1870. Danish National Art Library. The annotation lists colours, types of stone and other particulars; the sections to be reintegrated in the restored Gallery are clearly marked out. Note the asymmetries of the original facade that the Marble Gallery was meant to camouflage or, at least, make less clearly visible (cf. fig. 4.3). The drawing already has Meldahl's freely invented, central museum entrance and on the *piano nobile* all the windows have been realigned, but in the central bay, the window still retains the original type of triangular pediment. It was later replaced by an arch, so that the centre of the facade became far more imposing than it originally was (fig. 4.4).

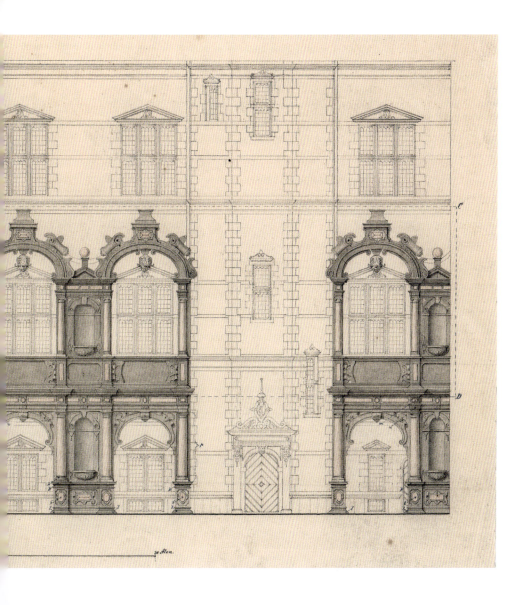

(as he himself put it) at "bringing the main castle back to the appearance it had in the days of Christian IV"[16] allowed the sculptor Christian Carl Peters to furnish replacements for the missing five statues that have nothing in the slightest in common with the pre-fire statuary.[17] More recent restorers have replaced these zinc figures with genuine sandstone replicas, but there has until recently been no attempt to go beyond Meldahl's careless practice in ignoring what can be gleaned from the post-fire remains as well as from the available descriptions from 1646 onwards.[18] The result is a mess that clashes problematically with Frederiksborg's modern function as a museum of national *history*.[19] It is to be hoped that the future will see a project to bring the castle exterior back as close as possible to what it would have looked like in c.1625.

It has, of course, not proved helpful that the wear and tear of time and weather prior to the fire had already done extensive damage. Part of the uppermost and very exposed series of statues had already disappeared by the early eighteenth century. Any reconstruction is therefore inevitably bedevilled with an element of uncertainty. However, by combining the early written and visual evidence with what is known about the manner and order in which artists of this period tended to put such statuary on display, it is possible to advance our knowledge about the original setup considerably.

A reappraisal of the evidence should commence with the Gallery itself, which – as we have seen – is an architectural afterthought striving to accommodate itself to the existing layout of the facade (fig. 4.14). Despite the odds, Hans van Steenwinckel and his aide Lorentz Sweys (or Sweis)[20] masterfully succeeded in giving the whole a clear and pleasant visual rhythm, with the figures six and seven as the basic module. On each of the two storeys, Tuscan below and Ionic above, seven bays crowned by arches, five in the central section, the bordering two each in their corners behind the stair turrets, frame windows and doors of the Royal Wing in a way that only in a few cases allows a revealing overlap to disclose the original asymmetry of the facade behind (fig. 4.3). The bays are fashioned in the manner of triumphal arches, with columns and exuberant, mannerist strapwork mouldings, each of these

FIG. 4.15. Ferdinand Meldahl, drawing and measuring of one of the arches of the Marble Gallery. The relief identifies this as the arch of Diana (cf. fig. 5.4). 1870. Danish National Art Library.

seven sections being set apart by niches adorned with a statue. The horizontal balustrade of the first-floor balcony is adorned with a series of reliefs, their differences in width (six relatively narrow, seven wider) dictated by the architecture and reflected in their differences of theme. Each of the six statue niches are crowned by a bulging, mannerist strapwork pediment, whereas the arching top of the upper seven bays serves as the basis for seven life-size, freestanding statues (fig. 4.15).

The Gallery's repeated six-seven modules are a key to understanding the original decorative scheme that was organised along a horizontal and vertical axis. The horizontal axis picks up and continues the plan of Steenwinckel's Terrace facade with a symmetrical and hierarchical, male-female pattern of distribution. By a strange paradox, this, the best preserved and most fully witnessed section of the Gallery, is also the least examined. It therefore seems useful briefly to recapitulate what is known about the original position of the Gallery's two lower series of a total of twelve statues.[21] These statues have always been relatively well sheltered from wind and rain, which goes far in explaining how Thurah in 1749 could affirm that the display was little changed since it had first been described by Berg in 1646.[22]

Mercury	Mars[23]	Venus	Orpheus	Eurydice	Ceres
Hercules	Pluto	**Proserpina**	Neptune	**Amphitrite**	Omphale

STAIR TURRETS

The names in bold refer to statues that survived the fire in 1859, if not complete then at least in a condition that gives us a reasonably clear picture of how the display was originally organised.[24]

The disposition is very like that of the Terrace: once again six pairs, but here three below and three above, all grouped symmetrically around the central axis, with, below, the monarch of Hades and his consort to the left and the Master of the Ocean and his queen to the

FIG. 4.16. Hendrick de Keyser with Gerrit Lambertsen, *Hercules,* c.1621, 167 cm. The Museum of National History at Frederiksborg.

right. At the end of the left row stood *Hercules*, whose *Omphale* was correspondingly situated at the end of the right row.

The well-preserved, handsomely energetic *Hercules* (fig. 4.16) shows clearly that he was meant for this original corner position. From here, behind the stair turret, he leans longingly forward to gain eye contact with his beloved *Omphale* in the opposite corner. Due to the protection provided by the corner, the expressive detail of his body has survived intact. The clear definition of his twisting torso and neck and the way his right hand grasps his club with such strength that the veins of his arm protrude gives a clear idea of the original's artistic qualities – but shows also how much most of these statues have suffered. Given its qualities, it is understandable that Meldahl moved the *Hercules* to a very prominent position, just to the left of the modern main entrance, at the centre of the Gallery. This is where the present writer first saw him, wondering what this could possibly mean in historical terms. Why would Christian IV and his advisors situate *Hercules* there? Others have asked the same, being misled by a pseudo-reconstruction that at no point admitted it was just that.[25]

Moreover, not only is this transfer unhistorical, but it has grave aesthetic consequences, since it deprives *Hercules'* body language of its original meaning. Standing right next to the central portal there is no need to lean forward and look diagonally across the courtyard, above all since Meldahl placed his beloved *Omphale* behind his back.

The Gallery's upper storey, slightly lower in height, repeats the pattern, with pairs from classical mythology framing the axis of symmetry. As on the facade of the Audience House (ch. VII), *Mars* and *Venus* were here joined by personifications of poetry and song, here *Orpheus* and his beloved *Eurydice*. Repeating the lower storey rhythm, these two pairs are then framed by a third, to the west *Mercury* and to the east *Ceres*. It is no doubt intentional that this chiastic positioning of figures personifying strength and power, trade and war gave the Gallery's western half that houses the king's stair turret a notably male preponderance, whereas beauty and poetry, plenty and sheer erotic dominance framed the queen's stair turret, thus allowing the Gallery, which, much like a mythological bridge, connects two life spheres, to mirror the way the Royal Wing was divided into two apartments, one for the monarch and the other for his queen.[26]

Here again it seems fruitful to reflect upon what the king had seen and, doubtless, admired during his visit to England. At the palace of Nonsuch (which like Theobalds has not survived), it is known that the dazzling facades of the great inner courtyard were adorned with three registers of decorations (one above the other) "of white stucco panels surrounded by borders of carved and gilded slate." Each of these registers were some 40 metres long. A diarist in the king's entourage was impressed by all this gilding – a feature that of course also became prominent at Frederiksborg. But while this is perhaps accidental, it is noteworthy that the visual programme of the Nonsuch facades likewise was gender specific in so far as the decoration of the king's western wing was all male and the queen's eastern wing correspondingly female, each with three times sixteen images with motifs drawn from either myth or allegory. In glittering gold and richly coloured, this was imagery easy to grasp and hard to forget – above all for a monarch eagerly looking out for ways in which to add magnificence to his new residence.[27]

IV · THE MARBLE GALLERY   85

FIG. 5.1. The Gallery at Güstrow, the palace of the Dukes of Mecklenburg in present-day Mecklenburg-Vorpommern. Completed c.1565 by Franz Parr.

V

The Seven Planet-Gods

I T IS FASCINATING TO SEE HOW THE ARTISTS AND their advisors succeeded in uniting this horizontal axis with the vertical, in which the number seven is fundamental. Why this is so emerges clearly from a book published in Amsterdam in 1631 (just a decade after the Gallery was completed) celebrating the memory of Hendrick de Keyser (fig. 5.2). With its programmatic title *Architectura moderna* the author, Salomon de Bray, aims to invest de Keyser with the role of the father of Dutch architecture. The book's focus is of course Dutch, but it also lists a project outside the Netherlands, to which the master and his workshop had delivered architectural frame and sculpture, namely the prestigious project of Steenwinckel for the "King of Denmark's Gallery at Frederiksborg." No doubt it was seen as a great honour that a foreign king had also applied for de Keyser's help.

FIG. 5.2. Hendrick de Keyser. Engraving by Joannes Meyssens, 1662.

FIG. 5.3. Illustration by Cornelis I. Danckerts in Salomon de Bray, *Architectura moderna*, Amsterdam 1631, plate xlii reproducing a drawing sent by Steenwinckel to Hendrick de Keyser to inform him about the planned "King of Denmark's Gallery at Frederiksborg."

What matters in the present context is that de Bray publishes and comments upon a drawing sent by Steenwinckel to inform de Keyser about the project (fig. 5.3). This is precious evidence, in fact the only surviving reference not only showing Steenwinckel's direct involvement, but also proving that Amsterdam was familiar with the quality of his work, surely because he had for an unknown period of time until 1613 worked and studied in the city, perhaps even in the master's studio.

Each of the Gallery's seven two-storey bays were, de Bray specifies, "dedicated (*toe-ge-eygent*) to one of the seven planet-gods", who, de Bray continues, were depicted twice in each bay, with "reliefs" (*beeldenisse*), surely the ones situated upon the first-floor balustrade, and with "a statue" (*het beeldt*) standing high on top of the second-storey vault, directly above the corresponding relief.[1]

In the drawing published by de Bray there are still no statues in the open niches (presumably they belong to a later phase in the project), but when seen together with de Bray's comments, the drawing illustrates clearly what plans there were with respect to the planet-gods.[2] On the balustrade, the reliefs of each of the seven bays were to represent the planet-gods' triumphal, seaborne chariots, a maritime variation of the typical *carro* imagery so common in Renaissance planet-god iconography (fig. 6.1).[3] Such maritime themes as seaborne gods and goddesses pervade much of the castle's iconography, a choice that here, as in the Forecourt and Tiltyard, probably alludes to Danish naval power.[4]

As for the statues on top of the arcades, the narrow section of the Gallery shown on Steenwinckel's drawing only has room for two bays, one with a god, the other with a goddess. The god, with crown, scep-

FIG. 5.4. Prints with planet-god symbolism in Cornelis I. Danckerts, *Nouveau Livre des/ Dieux et Deesses/ De la marine/ de l'jnventio/ de Henri de/ Caiser*, s.l. & a. [before 1656]: the chariots (from top to bottom) of Saturn, Mercury and Diana; for comparison, see fig. 5.6 and 5.3. Rijksmuseum, Amsterdam.

tre and emblematic eagle, can only be Jupiter. This identification is confirmed by the relief placed one storey below: in the Renaissance, the *carro* or chariot of Jupiter was typically drawn either by eagles or peacocks – and despite the drawing's diminutive format this chariot's team is clearly winged.

As for Steenwinckel's goddess, there are among planet-gods only two options: either Venus or Diana. The alluring veil, showing more than it covers, suggests Venus, an identification supported by her *carro*, which appears to be drawn by swans (her characteristic pigeons also occur, but these seem too large). Diana can

FIG. 5.5. Prints with planet-god symbolism in Iustus Danckerts, *Nouveau Livre des/ Dieux et Deesses/ De la marine/ de l'jnventio/ de Henri de/ Caiser,* s.l. & a. [after 1656]: the chariots (from top to bottom) of Jupiter, Venus, Apollo and Mars. This second edition was followed by a hitherto unacknowledged third edition from after 1656 that retains the original title and is held for instance by the Herzogin Anna Amalia Bibliothek in Weimar and the Victoria and Albert Museum in London. *Saturn* is in this final edition left out and the remainders renumbered. Rijksmuseum, Amsterdam.

confidently be discarded, since her typical *carro* was drawn either by virgins or a pair of deer (cf. fig. 4.15).[5]

Of all this only a limited number of fragmentary statues and reliefs have survived in the original. For a long time, therefore, uncertainty prevailed (un-

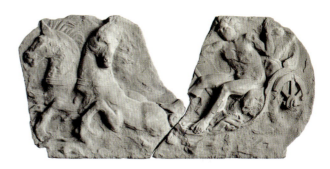

FIG. 5.6. The planet-god reliefs (some of them replaced by copies in the eighteenth century) that survived the fire were first repaired and cast in zinc and later recopied in stone. These copies of copies are still remarkably close to de Keyser's original drawings: here, for comparison, early photos (1870s?) with the chariots (from left to right) of Mercury, Jupiter, Diana, Venus and Apollo; for the original chariots of Mars and Saturn, see fig. 6.2–3. Danish National Art Library.

necessarily, as it happens) as to whether the planet-god project ever came to fruition.[6] This situation began to change in 1943, when the Dutch de Keyser expert Elisabeth Neurdenburg published a surprise discovery confirming that he in fact had delivered the balustrade's planet-god reliefs. In a private collection, she had found a rare series of prints by Cornelis I. Danckerts, an artist who had frequently collaborated with the great architect and had helped de Bray produce the *Architectura Moderna*. Neurdenburg accurately iden-

V · THE SEVEN PLANET-GODS   93

FIG. 5.7. Prints with sea-god symbolism in Cornelis I. Danckerts, *Nouveau Livre des/ Dieux et Deesses/ De la marine/ de l'jnventio/ de Henri de/ Caiser*, s.l. & a. [before 1656]; for comparison, see fig. 5.8. Rijksmuseum, Amsterdam.

tified these prints as reproductions of the master's original sketches for the reliefs at Frederiksborg, but she had no means of ascertaining whether the series was complete (fig. 5.4–7). Decades later, Meir Stein, a scholar of great iconographical acumen, spotted that these prints were, to a considerable degree, based upon traditional planet-god iconography (fig. 5.4–6). This confirmed de Bray's claim concerning the subject of

FIG. 5.8. The sea-god reliefs (most of them replaced in the eighteenth century) that survived the fire were first repaired and cast in zinc and later recopied in stone. These latter versions remain close to de Keyser's original drafts. Early photo (1870s?). Danish National Art Library.

the reliefs.[7] Renewed inspection of one of the surviving sets of these prints,[8] in the Rijksmuseum in Amsterdam, shows that the publication has no information as to their original purpose; and further, that the series in its original version had seven prints with planet-god symbolism (fig. 5.4–5) and five with all in all six sea-gods and sea-goddesses (fig. 5.7).[9]

The sculptors in de Keyser's workshop clearly followed the master's original drawings (which in the prints of course are inverted) down to the minutest detail: in the prints and the reliefs it is for instance only *Mars* and *Mercury* who have a zodiac traversing the horizon. As for the sea-gods and goddesses, however, only four of the designs reproduced in these prints were used for the Gallery (fig. 5.7–8) – but originally there may well have been more drawings to choose

V · THE SEVEN PLANET-GODS 95

from. What matters is that the prints are clear and independent evidence that these reliefs ultimately come from de Keyser's workshop; and further, that at least ten of the later replacements are faithful copies of the Dutch originals (fig. 5.6; 5.8).

As for the two prints without a match on the Gallery there is no way of determining whether de Keyser – as seems plausible – had drawn alternative suggestions that for some reason are not included in the prints. The disparity may of course also be due to eighteenth-century restorers, who in these two cases chose to differ from the originals, when replacing old reliefs with new, but what argues against this is that the style is so similar.

In any case, de Keyser had clearly studied the iconography of the planets closely.[10] In the period, the motif was hugely popular. This was imagery linking Cosmos above and the Order below, and this in a way that transcended confessional borders. This was no doubt one of the reasons why the planet-god theme, with a certain degree of iconographical variation, was remarkably widely applied. For the influential decorative programmes of the Medici Palazzo Pitti and the Versailles of Louis XIV this symbolism would of course later in the century become an essential component,[11] but in the early decades of the seventeenth century it had long since established itself as a stable component in festive pageants[12] and in sculpture,[13] fresco,[14] painting,[15] tapestries[16] as well as in prints[17] and such modest art forms as wood carving on the facades of North German timber dwellings.[18]

For the reliefs of *Saturn*, *Mercury*, *Diana*, *Mars* and *Apollo*,[19] traditional, fairly straightforward iconography is applied;[20] *Venus*'s dolphins rather than doves drawing her chariot are unusual, but not without parallels, for instance in representations of Venus Marina; for the

FIG. 5.9. The central section of Meldahl's reconstructed Gallery, c.1904. Danish National Art Library.
Statues of *Hercules* and *Pluto* (both misplaced) frame the arch of the lower tier, *Venus* and *Orpheus* that of the tier above. On the balustrade de Keyser's reliefs with sea-gods frame a planet-god chariot, *in casu* of *Apollo* (also misplaced). On top of the arch above the planet-god relief one would originally have had the corresponding statue, *in casu* of *Apollo* himself – but in Meldahl's reconstruction we get *Venus*. Truly a mess!

bulls dragging *Jupiter*'s chariot I have found no parallels, but given his legendary rape of Europa, this erotic twist to the motif is, in a context not unwilling to dwell on this aspect of human nature, easily comprehensible. And since, as we shall see (ch. VI), this relief was meant

V · THE SEVEN PLANET-GODS 97

FIG. 5.10. Lauritz de Thurah (1706–59). Portrait by Johan Hörner, c.1750, oil on canvas, 80 × 63. The Museum of National History at Frederiksborg. The son of a bishop, Thurah was educated in the army's Corps of Royal Engineers. Travels through Europe gave him first-hand knowledge of the High Baroque in England, France, Italy, Austria and Saxony (1729–31). Back in Denmark he received numerous royal commissions, his work as an architect culminating with the landmark twisted spire of Our Saviour's Church in Copenhagen (1749–52). Thurah being a man of learning and energy, King Christian VI entrusted him with the task of compiling and editing a monumental survey of Danish architecture in Danish, German and French. *Den danske Vitruvius I–II* was edited in Copenhagen 1746–49; Thurah's fundamental discussion of the antiquities of the capital, *Hafnia Hodierna* was published in 1748, intended to celebrate the tercentenary of the royal dynasty.

to occupy the position right at the centre of the balcony, the very bulk of the bulls gives it all the required weight.

As for the gender shift from the male *Mars* and *Apollo* to the consistent use of bare-breasted female drivers for the rest of the chariots, this is unusual, but seems to go back to Steenwinckel himself; in the drawing published by de Bray in 1631, the drivers of *Venus*' and *Jupiter*'s chariots are likewise female (cf. fig. 5.3). The reason may well be that we are dealing with an aesthetic that significantly prefers female beauty, in fact only offering room for a pair of male drivers in the reliefs originally (see ch. VI) framing the queen's (by 1619 the *maitresse en titre*'s) stair turret.

Turning from the reliefs to the planet-god statues that originally stood high on top of the arcades (fig. 5.9), one first needs to underline that apart from de Bray's testimony from 1631 we are otherwise left completely in the dark here. Indeed, the account by Berg from 1646 leaves the seven statues unidentified. This is where the evidence from Lauritz de Thurah, the great eighteenth-century architect and antiquarian, becomes crucial (fig. 5.10). In his monumental survey of the nation's architecture, *Den danske Vitruvius* ("The Danish Vitruvius") from 1746–49, he enumerates all the statues (fig. 5.11). But based on his list, no living soul would have guessed that the Gallery's top section might once have been devoted to the planets.

Thurah names six of the statues (of which the four printed in bold are at least partly extant): Cybele,

FIG. 5.11. Frederiksborg as displayed in one of the plates (no. x) in Lauritz de Thurah's *Den danske Vitruvius,* vol. II, Copenhagen 1749.

Saturn, Bacchus, **Juno**, **Jupiter** and **Minerva** – as for the seventh and final statue, he had no idea who it represented.[21]

Since the classic group of planet-gods counts as follows: **Saturn**, Apollo (= Sun), Diana (= Luna), **Jupiter**, Venus, Mercury and Mars, the discrepancy, be it with or without the unidentified seventh, is glaring. In fact, only *Saturn* and *Jupiter* (both extant) are common to both lists.

The question therefore arises whether, as Neurdenburg, Stein and, most recently, the historian Thomas Lyngby have argued, there was at some point a complete change in the project, the planet-god theme therefore being abandoned.[22] Or, alternatively, whether the statues seen by Thurah were only in part the originals.

Everything indicates that the latter is the case. First, because there is a disturbing, not to say suspicious, lack of order and logic in the mythological assembly seen by Thurah on top of the Gallery. Thurah can be relied upon, if not in absolutely every detail then at least generally. As shown by his wide-ranging and still fundamental antiquarian and topographical publications on the architecture and antiquities of Denmark, he typically knew what was what. And the assembly he describes cannot possibly have been set up by Steenwinckel, whose adherence to well-ordered symmetry is otherwise well documented. Secondly, the presence of *Saturn* eating one of his children is a motif that in this period almost invariably denotes the planets. And this brilliantly contorted statue is, it is commonly agreed, unmistakably from de Keyser's workshop (fig. 5.12). As shown by the (hitherto overlooked) remnants in his left hand, he was – as was traditional (fig. 5.13) – originally holding a scythe, probably in gilded metal.[23] Its horizontal shaft would of course further

FIG. 5.12. Hendrick de Keyser with Gerrit Lambertsen, *Saturn*, c.1621, 176 cm. The Museum of National History at Frederiksborg.

FIG. 5.13. *Saturn with his scythe*, c.1650, marble relief by Artus Quellinus. Amsterdam, Koninklijk Paleis (Stadhuis). In the left hand of de Keyser's *Saturn* (fig. 5.12) there are hitherto unobserved traces of a scythe held in similar fashion.

have emphasised his torso's twisted *figura serpentinata*. Third, Amsterdam is, it is commonly agreed, also the provenance of the only other statue that would fit into a group of planet-gods, namely the no less brilliant *Jupiter* (fig. 5.14). And this statue is, again uniquely, of

V · THE SEVEN PLANET-GODS   101

FIG. 5.14. Hendrick de Keyser with Gerrit Lambertsen, *Jupiter*, c.1621, 177 cm. The Museum of National History at Frederiksborg.

almost exactly the same height and proportions as that of *Saturn*.

Of the group seen by Thurah, two more statues have survived. Of these *Minerva* is clearly an outsider. Not only is she not a planet-god, but she is in style very different from the two others and, crucially, almost 30 cm taller[24] – a disproportion suggesting that her original context was very different. As for her original

FIG. 5.15. Hendrick de Keyser with Gerrit Lambertsen, *Venus*, c.1621, 184 cm. The Museum of National History at Frederiksborg.

provenance, it is a fair guess that it was only in the 1730s, during extensive repairs of the castle, that *Minerva* was given her new position among the seven statues on top of the Gallery.[25] At this point only a history-conscious connoisseur like Thurah would have cared about adhering to an original programme.

Unlike the mediocre *Minerva* it is, on the other hand, commonly agreed that the Amsterdam workshop is

FIG. 5.16. Hendrick de Keyser with Gerrit Lambertsen, *Venus*, c.1621. Detail showing the goats at her feet. The Museum of National History at Frederiksborg.

FIG. 5.17. The goddess Venus with her goat: Vincenzo Cartari, *Le imagini de i dei degli antichi*, Lyon 1581.

also where the fourth of the original statues from the top of the Gallery comes from. This elegantly fluid statue, bowing forward – as if in happy acknowledgement of the admiration of mortal spectators – has, since Thurah, been identified as Juno or, alternatively, as Cybele, but neither are planet-gods.[26]

However, this identification is by no means certain. The fact that she is slightly taller than *Jupiter* and *Saturn* does not necessarily indicate that she is foreign to the group. With his (now missing) arm lifted, doubtless holding golden thunderbolts, *Jupiter* would have been at least as tall. Her proportions and style are, it is commonly agreed, very like that of de Keyser's *Jupiter* and *Saturn*. Indeed, nothing stands in the way of accepting her as part of the original ensemble (fig. 5.15).

What remains problematic is her identity. Her gesture of holding on to her breast has led to the hypothesis that she is either a Juno or Ops. Associated with both these goddesses are myths relating how the Firmament's Milky Way was created from milk from their breasts.[27] This of course establishes a connection of sorts with the planet-god myths, but not a conclusive one. Moreover, the question is whether this identification is cogent. Holding a hand up to the breast is not a gesture exclusive to these deities. And at the feet of this statue is a goat with twisted horns; behind her right leg are the remains of a second such goat or heifer (fig. 5.16). These animals have no connection with Juno and Ops (let alone Cybele, with whom the statue has also been identified). But in the period's mythological handbooks the goat or heifer with its characteristic horns is a standard attribute of Venus in her role as the emphatically sensual Venus Epitragia (fig. 5.17).[28] Moreover, ancient and renaissance statues, prints and paintings of Venus often show her holding a hand in front of her breast. Since everything indicates that this statue comes from the Amsterdam workshop, it is reasonable to assume that we have here a third member of de Keyser's original group of planet-gods.

To conclude: in overwhelming detail the evidence confirms that de Keyser did in fact deliver as originally ordered. De Bray was his friend and wrote within a decade of de Keyser's workshop producing the statues and reliefs for the gallery: despite recent claims to the opposite, his report from 1631 – along with otherwise surviving early evidence – surely outranks the list offered by Thurah in 1749, more than a century later. Not only does all the surviving early evidence, be it verbal or graphic (fig. 5.4–5), sculptural (fig. 5.6; 6.2–3) or architectural (fig. 5.3), converge in support of this conclusion, but so do all the *original*[29] parts of the top assembly of statues (fig. 5.12; 5.14–15) – and given the nature of the stone in which they were carved and the climate to which they were exposed, such limited survival (three out of seven) is, as experts tell me, only what might be expected. What Thurah saw, when compiling his text for this section (probably in the late 1730s), was therefore partly original and partly the result of more recent restoration. And as we shall presently see, the disposition of the statues was already then almost totally wrong.

The century between Thurah and the fire in 1859 only added to this confusion. As shown by drawings and a painting dated June 1858, a year and a half before the fire, as well as by a drawing by Meldahl shortly after the fire, restorers had at some point after Thurah once again taken the top statues down and, when putting them back up, once again repositioned *Saturn*, who

FIG. 5.18. Photo of the Gallery just after the fire in December 1859 (detail). On top of the partially preserved Gallery, the second statue from the left, or west, is clearly *Jupiter*, standing precisely where the painter Frederik Christian Lund had seen and drawn him in June 1858. Antikvarisk-Topografisk Arkiv, The National Museum of Denmark.

now was third from the east, whereas *Jupiter* now was second from the west. This is also where a precious just-after-the-fire photo (fig. 5.18) shows *Jupiter* still standing high.[30]

FIG. 6.1. Johann Sadeler after Maerten de Vos, *The Planet-God Saturn*. From a series of engravings from 1581.

VI

Jupiter and the King

THE DESTRUCTIVE HAVOC OF TIME, CLIMATE, fire and the, no doubt, well-meaning efforts of restorers makes it difficult to determine in which order Steenwinckel had planned to set up his group of planet-gods. The print published by de Bray (fig. 5.3) says little about the final appearance of the statues, but as to their position it gives a precious hint: *Venus* is placed on *Jupiter*'s left. When taking Steenwinckel's well-documented preference for visual symmetry into account, it is a reasonable guess that on his right Jupiter would have had *Diana*, the group's only other goddess, whereas the remaining four males would have been positioned two and two, on either side of this central trio.

This assumption seems to be borne out by a second circumstance. The de Bray print's seaborne *carri* of Jupiter and Venus (fig. 5.3) are both driving in the same direction, from left to right or, if you prefer, from east to west. In the extant reliefs, there are, in addition to *Jupiter* and *Venus*, only two gods driving in the same direction, namely *Apollo* and *Mars*. By a happy coincidence, the original position of the *Mars* (likewise considered to be an original from the Amsterdam workshop) happens to be known (fig. 6.2): after the fire in 1859 it was found in what seems to have been its original place, at the easternmost end of the balustrade,[1] a fact which allows us tentatively to infer that the original east-towards-west order of the planet-gods was MARS, APOLLO, VENUS and, in the middle, JUPITER.

For the sake of symmetry, one would expect the remaining *carri* to drive, or rather sail, in the opposite direction. This is in fact also the case. Not only *Diana* (cf. fig. 4.15), but also *Mercury* and *Saturn* are sailing from west towards east, in the direction of central Jupiter. It is a fair guess that the order from west to east

FIG. 6.2. Hendrick de Keyser with Gerrit Lambertsen, *The Chariot of Mars*, c.1621, 79 × 176. Early photo: Danish National Art Library.

FIG. 6.3. Hendrick de Keyser with Gerrit Lambertsen, *The Chariot of Saturn*, c.1621, 79 × 176. Early photo: Danish National Art Library.

of this group was SATURN, MERCURY and DIANA, first because Saturn usually leads off such planet-god series and second because the original relief is the only other to have been at least partly preserved, probably because it was originally positioned *vis-à-vis* that of *Mars*, in the well-protected west corner, just behind the stair turret (fig. 6.3). After *Saturn*, Steenwinckel would have placed *Mercury*, so that *Diana* could have the place next to *Jupiter* and *Venus* that on his other side, a figurative constellation of female-male-female that highlights the crowning centrality of *Jupiter*, the god in whose hands everything comes together.

With the planet-gods positioned in this order, there is an aspect that suddenly makes sense. The original, central gateway leading into the castle's Inner Courtyard has a diminutive Jupiter positioned on top, which

VI · JUPITER AND THE KING   111

in telling detail (the god straddling the eagle below and holding his thunderbolts (fig. 2.7)) anticipates the *Jupiter* of the Gallery; on the portal's top rear there is yet a *Jupiter* (fig. 6.4), for which Steenwinckel is the master, an arrangement that, on this reading, would have reached its final, soaring culmination on top of the original Gallery, where the king of the Gods would have been standing in the centre, flanked by three planet-gods on either side. Here, from above, de Keyser's *Jupiter* seems to echo de Vries' *Neptune* in raising his right arm, no doubt originally holding golden thunderbolts high in a commanding gesture of welcome.[2]

There is plenty of evidence that this was how de Keyser's *Jupiter* originally looked. Numerous Dutch and Italian prints show Jupiter in a similar posture, but

FIG. 6.4. Hans van Steenwinckel, *Jupiter holding the Globe*, c.1619. Relief situated above the main gate into the Inner Courtyard at Frederiksborg.

FIG. 6.5. Philips Galle, *The planet-god Jupiter*. Engraving from 1586 showing one of the life-size planet-gods in bronze made by Jacques Jonghelinck for Alessandro Farnese, Duke of Parma. British Museum, London.

112 · VI · JUPITER AND THE KING

in the present context there is a contemporary parallel that comes remarkably close. In 1585, following a long siege, Antwerp was forced to surrender to the Spanish viceroy, Alessandro Farnese. In an act of homage, the city "celebrated" the duke's entry by presenting him with a costly group of bronze statues representing the seven planet-gods. This almost life-size ensemble was the work of the Flemish sculptor Jacques Jonghelinck (fig. 6.5). During the Duke's entry, it was set up in front of the Antwerp City Hall in the market square (*Groote Markt*). The group, which today adorns the Throne Room of the Royal Palace in Madrid, was in its own day renowned, and a series of prints makes it possible to study its iconography.[3] When Hendrick de Keyser received the commission from the Danish king for a series of life-size planet-gods, there are clear indications that he and his workshop took a close look at the prints illustrating the only parallel, recently commissioned in the Netherlands. Like the *Jupiter* of Jonghelinck, that of de Keyser sits atop of the eagle and puts his left arm down to his hip, whereas he with his right doubtless would have held his golden thunderbolts high. What could celebrate the prowess of the Emperor Charles v's grandson would probably also appeal to a Christian IV whose imperial ambitions in precisely these years became a guiding star for his, as it would emerge, catastrophic foreign policy.[4]

After the Danish victory in the war with Sweden in 1611–13, the decoration of Frederiksborg is characterised by almost dizzying ambition. As we shall see in the final section, the Tiltyard with its central arch bears clear, but long forgotten, allusions to the Imperial Palace in Rome. Prior to examining this evidence, it seems useful briefly to summarise how the castle presented itself to its visitors through a series of dazzling *tableaux* of ever increasing splendour, first with de Vries' Neptune fountain, then the double columns with antiquity's two greatest conquerors and behind them the glittering array of two times six gods and heroes framing the portal with the insignia of the king and queen. In the Inner Courtyard, the Gallery, finally, has two narratives. One that in chiastic rhythm frames the stair turrets of the king and queen with an emphasis on the male and female dimension and another, rising above the centrally positioned rulers of the seas and the underworld, that is crowned, as it were, by the Gallery summit's assembly of planet-god deities with Jupiter in the middle, an assembly symbolic of the postulated links between the Danish monarchy and the cosmic order determining events in all the crucial spheres of human life. In the days of King Christian this narrative was then taken up and brought to culmination in the royal Audience Chamber, where the ceiling was adorned with gilded reliefs of planet-gods on their *carri*.[5]

Truly, this was a time of hubris.

FIG. 7.1. Heinrich Beust, *Christian IV at his coronation riding at the ring*, 1598, gilded silver. The rider is 71.5 cm, the columns 130 cm tall. The Royal Danish Collection, Rosenborg.

VII

The Royal Tiltyard and the Imperial Palace of Rome

THE IMPRESSION THAT THIS WAS A TIME OF hubris is reinforced when one leaves the castle itself and turns west to inspect what is left of the Royal Tiltyard.

To understand this extension of the compound that dates from c.1614, brief mention should be made of the Tiltyard's surroundings (fig. 1.5; 7.2–3). To the east one had the castle moat and to the west the Kitchen-and-Stables Wing, which goes back to the days of the king's father; to the north the Tiltyard was closed in by yet another architectural afterthought, the Privy Gallery that elegantly spans the moat and reaches the otherwise completely freestanding Audience House at its end. French architecture has several similar galleries spanning a moat. As shown by Mette Bligaard, the decoration with stags' heads has clear French parallels. But as rightly observed by Emily Cole,

FIG. 7.2. The Privy Gallery and the Audience House at Frederiksborg. Ground plan from 1836 showing the disposition of the first-floor rooms under and after Christian IV. Danish National Art Library.

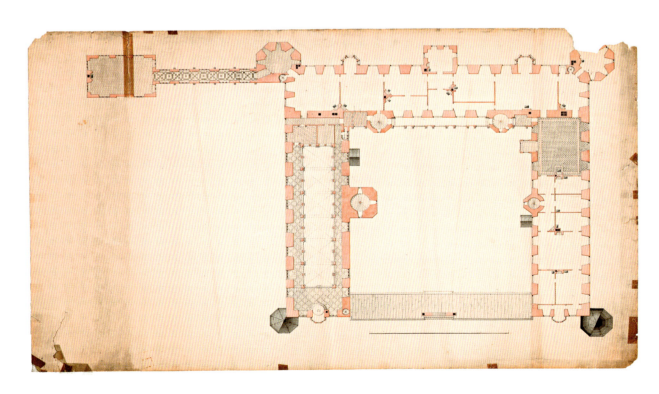

118 · VII · THE ROYAL TILTYARD AND THE IMPERIAL PALACE OF ROME

FIG. 7.3. The Privy Gallery and the Audience House at Frederiksborg. The facade is seen from the south with the moat and Chapel Wing to the right and the Stables to the left.

"French Long Galleries generally lead nowhere, whereas the passage at Frederiksborg … served as a through route to the Audience Chamber."

So also here it seems relevant to reflect on what King Christian had actually seen of comparable structures. As suggested by Simon Thurley, the way the so-called Cross Gallery reached out from the main corpus of Queen Anne's Somerset House to the freestanding Closet at its end is a very similar solution, be it coincidental or the result of otherwise unrecorded plans being sent back and forth.[1] However, when Christian saw his sister's gallery, his own was already well under way. Still, the comparison merits consideration, because during his earlier visit, in 1606, the king also saw, for instance, the palace at Greenwich, where he was lodged in a gallery overlooking the tiltyard (ch. III).

VII · THE ROYAL TILTYARD AND THE IMPERIAL PALACE OF ROME   119

And at Richmond (where he also lodged), an almost four-hundred-foot long two-storey gallery with windows on the one side facing the river Thames and on the other the Privy Garden and Orchard connected the main palace with a Banqueting House at the palace's outer perimeter. Indeed, this was one of Richmond Palace's immediately striking architectural aspects.[2] Whitehall Palace, where King Christian also stayed, offers a further, even more suggestive parallel. Here, the palace's two sections divided by King Street were linked by a gallery traversing the street through the upper part of the Holbein Gate. Access to this gallery was from the two-storeyed Privy Gallery, which on the opposite side of King Street was continued by a gallery overlooking Whitehall's Tiltyard.[3]

Finally, there is, once again, the impact of Theobalds to consider. As Emily Cole has very recently made clear, the projecting gallery range reaching from Theobalds' south facade out into the Great Garden originally had a tower at its end, the tower providing lodgings for such prestigious guests as Queen Elizabeth's dazzling favourites, the Earl of Leicester and, later, the Earl of Essex (fig. 3.8).[4] Along with the royal quarters, this may well have been some of the best lodgings that the palace had on offer. So perhaps this was also where King Christian was accommodated during his visit. In any case, there are some highly suggestive elements here, such as (i) a gallery reaching out to a prestigious, freestanding edifice and (ii) a gallery combined with a bridge and a tiltyard: the use of this and similar galleries in Tudor residences may well have been remembered by King Christian and eventually put to effective use by his master builders.

For King Christian and his master builders there were, however, other possible models of inspiration, such as the Long Gallery (*Der lange Gang*) in Dresden. Standing above an open, ground-floor loggia with twenty-one arches, this closed gallery connected the Electoral Residence with the richly furnished Stables, the latter a quasi-museum displaying the riches of the elector and his stupendous assembly of horses often featuring in competitions in the Tiltyard.[5]

But whatever the inspiration(s) for the Privy Gallery at Frederiksborg, a structure completely unparalleled in Danish architecture, attention has rightly been drawn to the decision to give these facades a uniform sandstone facing, which handsomely sets off the new complex from the main red-brick bulk of the castle (fig. 7.3). A new awareness of materials is already in evidence here, years before the instalment of the Marble Gallery (chs. IV–VI). The resulting 19 metres long complex of Privy Gallery and Audience House elegantly closes in the Tiltyard while at the same time leading out to the park. A parallel with Dresden also suggests itself here: using a gateway as the foundation for a freestanding, richly ornamented and sandstone-covered, separate wing of a palace is what the Saxon electors had created with their *Georgenbau*. Their Danish in-law may well be following their lead here. The geometric structuring of the harmonious facades seems so sophisticated that some have detected the hand of an Inigo Jones – but this seems implausible.[6]

In any case, it seems worth the while to consider what the motivation was behind this extension. In my view, it was probably the realisation, by the king and his advisors, that, by 1606, for all their rich furnishings his so-called double apartment lodgings were hopelessly old-fashioned. This layout with the king and queen inhabiting each their own adjoining half of the *piano nobile* was much used in Scandinavian manor houses

FIG. 7.4. The Audience Chamber at Frederiksborg. After a fire in 1665, the grandson of Christian IV refurnished the chamber in splendid style. The chamber holds portraits of all the Royal ancestors back to Christian I, the central painting on the south wall showing Christian V flanked by his sons and successor.

and residences, a very early example being the lodgings from 1537 of King Christian's grandfather at *Malmøhus* in Scania – but in the modern, more ceremonial court life such compact layout was problematic in as far as it did not allow the solemn arrival of an envoy or princely guest to be orchestrated as a procession through a series of chambers of increasing splendour. Entering from the king's stair turret one was immediately standing in his drawing room, as it were. This is very similar to how the lodgings of the king's grandfather Duke Ulrich of Mecklenburg had been fashioned in his palace at Güstrow in the 1560s – but court life had since then become more sophisticated. The monarch's apartment left no room for the kind of ceremonial entrance that (as French etiquette by now prescribed) across four rooms finally took the visitor into the Royal presence.

Danish court ceremonial was different from the French. As at German courts it was closer to the so-called Burgundian tradition, with its stronger separation of the monarch's private and public sphere. Still, the period's increasing emphasis on architectural distance between the monarch and the audience-seeker seems to be what in this case motivated architectural change.[7] A separate, more monumental, ceremonially suitable space for audiences with a correspondingly dazzling route of access had to be provided – as indeed it was, the new route taking the visitor through the by now almost obligatory sequence of rooms, first through the two halls adjoining the stairs, then through the tower chamber and the gallery that both had splendid views, to the north of the lake and the park and, to the south, of the Tiltyard – at which point the visitor was finally admitted into royal presence (fig. 7.2). The audience chamber of Christian IV was lost in a fire in 1665, but the present, avowedly baroque, replacement

FIG. 7.5. Frederiksborg. The Arch of the Tiltyard and the Audience House.

from c.1675[8] is rich compensation and very similar in dimensions (fig. 7.4).

It is time to turn to the richly adorned Tiltyard that in 1614 was laid out right beneath the windows of the Privy Gallery and the Audience House, partly no doubt to maximise the impact of the vistas and spectacles seen by those approaching the king; this is an effect

FIG. 7.6. Peder Hansen Resen (1625–88) was a high-ranking civil servant and professor, highly renowned as a historian of Danish law and as a collector of manuscripts, books and prints. As the first ever editor and translator of Snorre's *Edda* he was a pioneer in giving learned Europe access to the Norse heritage. An antiquarian of remarkable range, he established collections of copies, maps, drawings and data upon which the first complete topographical description of Denmark, the *Atlas Danicus*, was based. Engraving by I. Cramer Hass from 1753. The Royal Danish Library.

very similar to what King Christian would have experienced during his visits to London and to Dresden. At the palace in Greenwich, he had been lodged and "feasted … most royally" in the "two great towers and galleries within the Tilt-Yard", where the space was so ample, an eyewitness reports, that not even "the vaine gazers (in which our nation is more rich than any kingdome)" found any "want of their foolish eyes satisfaction." And in Dresden, where the Long Gallery (*Der lange Gang*) linking the residence with the stables offers similar views of the splendid *Turnierhof* below, the role of the tiltyard as a setting for ceremonial display was equally strongly pronounced. By no means the only aspect that recalls Dresden (see below), tiltyards were in the period an almost indispensable part of a royal residence (fig. 7.5), on the Continent as well as in England. In view of its overall importance to King Christian's image, it is therefore surprising how little has hitherto been done to understand its original layout.[9]

To understand the "message" that such a field would convey we should listen attentively to what the learned Peder Hansen Resen states (fig. 7.6). Not only was Resen his period's leading authority on Danish topography, but he wrote within two generations of Steenwinckel finishing the Tiltyard. His great *Atlas Danicus* was moreover based upon hundreds of reports and outlines sent to him from contributors throughout the country.[10] What he offers is, along with the Steenwinckel drawing (fig. 5.3) and the description by Berg from 1646, firsthand evidence concerning ideas and discourses about Frederiksborg that were then current. When turning to describe Frederiksborg's Tiltyard, this is what he, in a translation of his original Latin, comments:

"Add to all this a field of jousting laid out for the games called Trojan (*lusibus...Troianis*): there one may behold a magnificent building (*splendidam ... aedem*), which is called the Judgement's House (*aedem judicii*), artful arches, gilded obelisks, huge sculptures, statues representing gods and goddesses, all fashioned in so fortunate an emulation of antiquity, that the Greek

FIG. 7.7. Caspar Fincke, grill decoration for the Tiltyard Arch at Frederiksborg, 1616.

and Roman past, now defeated by the art of the modern age, almost must redden with shame over its own products."[11]

When describing a royal residence, an element of panegyric was of course obligatory. In Resen's case, it results in a telling paradox: here, the modern age no longer emulates antiquity: it has surpassed it. If we hold on to this comparison, there are aspects that, when seen in context, will prove highly revealing. But setting aside for the moment what the reference to the games as *Trojan* might imply, it will, to begin with, prove useful to compare it with the roughly contemporary and, in every respect, closely related tiltyards in Dresden (1586–91), Berlin (1590s) and, of course, Copenhagen (1596).[12] These were tiltyards that King Christian himself had seen; he had visited Berlin in 1592 and 1595 and

VII · THE ROYAL TILTYARD AND THE IMPERIAL PALACE OF ROME   127

FIG. 7.8. Running at the ring in front of the Berlin *Schloss* in 1592. Modern facsimile after print in *Historicae relationis continuatio 1593* by Jacob Francus. In the centre foreground is a temporary *Judicirhaus*, visible behind which are the three parallel lanes with the arch of the ring at the centre of the middle lane. This arch is crowned by a statue of Fortuna holding a banner inscribed *Victoria*. In the background is the Berlin Castle with spectators standing in front as well as in all the windows.

Dresden in 1597. These visits gave the king models to emulate and connoisseurs with whom to discuss his own projects. Contemporaries knew King Christian to be an eager and successful tiltyard man (fig. 7.7).[13] For his own permanent field at Frederiksborg he would therefore have aimed for the best, and in this respect, there can be little doubt that the magnificent enclosed *Turnierhof* in Dresden was the prime example of what he now wanted his architect to produce. In Dresden, the Elector Christian I had, in Latin, proclaimed it his object to provide "a stable for his horses" (EQVORVM STATIONI) and an "adjoining field/for military exercises" (AREAMQVE ADIVNCTAM/MILITARIVM EXERCITATIONVM CAVSSA) – now it was Denmark's turn to build something similar.[14] The differences between the Dresden and Frederiksborg tiltyards are of course obvious, but as we shall see, there are, or rather *were*, notable parallels, too.

To begin with, it will prove useful briefly to recapitulate what kind of field this activity and its participants would demand. As shown by two contemporary prints, one from 1593 (fig. 7.8) depicting a running at the ring on the *Rennplatz* or *Stechbahn*[15] in front of the Berlin residence of the Elector Johann Georg[16] (from where Christian IV brought home his queen and where he himself participated in runnings at the ring) and the other showing a similar competition during his own coronation festivities in 1596 (fig. 7.9),[17] where the Dresden sculptor and tiltyard expert Giovanni Maria Nosseni[18] was brought along to help with the planning, such tiltyards typically consisted of a course divided into three lanes. In the first of the side lanes, the participants were lined up, all decked out in sumptuous apparel; in the central lane, they ran at the ring, and in the side lane further back they then rode off to dismount.

FIG. 7.9. Running at the ring at Amagertorv in Copenhagen at the coronation of Christian IV in 1596 (lower section of the original). From *Dennemärckische Krönung. Das ist, Kurtze doch gründliche beschreibung, mit was ceremonien ... die Krönung Christiani des IV ... verrichtet ... worden*, [Frankfurt an der Oder] 1597. Clearly visible in the foreground are the three lanes of the *Stechbahn* with the columns of the central arch (designed by Giovanni Maria Nosseni?) in the middle. The caption reads *Ringelrennen und Aufzug Kön. May. in Dennemarck zu Koppenhagen vom 3 biss auff den 6. Septembris A(nn)o. 96 mit grosser Herrlichkeit gehalten* ("The running at the ring and procession of his Royal Majesty in Copenhagen performed with great pomp from 3 until 6 September (15)96"). The Royal Danish Library.

In the *Turnierhof* in Dresden, along with that of Frederiksborg, one of the oldest preserved monuments of its kind in Europe, the position of Nosseni's original bronze pillars illustrate how the field could be divided into three lanes of equal width, a procedure brought vividly to life by the hooks on the pillars to which such ropes were originally attached.

At Frederiksborg this three-lane layout meant that contestants would have entered from the castle's Forecourt, line up in the southern end of the course, with each contestant then riding forward, one at a time,

FIG. 7.10. The king shows off: saddle, spurs and reins used by Christian IV at the running at the ring in 1634 during the festivities in connection with the wedding of his son and heir to Magdalena Sibylla, daughter of the Elector of Saxony. Pearl embroidery by a group of seventeen artisans directed by one Gert Osserjan. Silks, pearls, gold, enamel and diamonds, 1634, max. length 96.5, width 130 cm. The Royal Danish Collection, Rosenborg.

along the lane adjoining the moat as far as the Audience House, where they would turn to ride south, up through the middle lane towards the arch. If successful in hitting the ring, they would then proceed to the *Judicirhaus* to prove their claim and, then or later, receive their reward. For all contestants, the exit route would be the side lane parallel with the Kitchen and Stables, down towards the Audience House and out through its gateway, there to dismount.

This circuitous, trifold route gave ample time for spectators to admire the participants, who flaunted their magnificent attire, their gowns of shining silks and velvet, their stirrups, saddles and horse apparel gleaming with pearls, amethysts and gold (fig. 7.10). Apart from the prowess in hitting the ring, this "cat walk" aspect was very much what it was all about. As an

FIG. 7.11. *Prægtigt Optog til et Carroussel ved den udvalgte Prinds Christian den Vs Formæling med Prindsesse Magdalena Sybilla af Churhuset Saxen i Octb. 1634 paa Amager Torv* ("Festive procession in a carousel at Amagertorv in October 1634 during the celebration of the Crown Prince Elect Christian v's wedding to the princess of the Elector's House of Saxony"). At the parade, the king and his heir were dressed up as Scipio Africanus and Scipio Asiaticus. Engraving by Christophorus Swenckius after drawing by Chrispijn de Passe, Copenhagen 1634, 38 × 48. The Royal Danish Library.

English eyewitness reports from joustings in Greenwich in 1606: "the King of Denmarke (was) armed very rich, and mounted on a most stately courser" (fig. 7.10).[19] Showing off riches and equipment that, in Frederiksborg as in Dresden, was kept assembled for permanent display in a nearby treasure house with access for the privileged few was a way of boosting the royal "reputation" (to quote a concept vital for understanding the king's attitude).[20]

In tiltyards, arches were typically situated centrally in respect to the spectators and judges. In Berlin, the spectators looked on from the castle (fig. 7.8) and in Dresden (fig. 7.12) from the "Long Gallery" (*Der lange Gang*), either below its arches or from its first-floor windows; in Frederiksborg, finally, the restricted space dictated a new solution, the spectators looking on from the castle's windows, from those of the Chapel, of the Great Hall, of the Privy Gallery and of the Audience House.

In Dresden and on the self-celebrating statue showing King Christian at his coronation (fig. 7.1), the "arch" was in fact a set of columns, but in Copenhagen, at his coronation, in Berlin and at Frederiksborg it was a proper arch with statues on top, the apparatus in both cases indicating where the ring was positioned or, rather, suspended. In all four residences there was a fixed spot for the judges to sit, in Dresden in a designated three-window box just above the arch, and in Berlin in a temporary *Judizierhäuschen* ("little Judge-House") close to where the columns or arch were standing.[21] Frederiksborg also had a *Judicirhaus* ("Judge-House"), "a splendid building",[22] not in the middle, but at the southern short end, where it rounded off the field, thus no doubt giving the complex a welcome aesthetic unity. Berg and Resen agree that it was a splendid edifice,

apparently decked out with figures and reliefs that would have served as a counterpoint to the still extant, richly decorated Audience House at the opposite end of the *Rennbahn*.²³

As to the appearance of this *Judicirhaus* we are, however, sadly ill-informed. Meldahl pulled it down completely in 1865, an act for which he has rightly been severely criticised, since he thereby ruined the Tiltyard's original enclosure (fig. 7.13).²⁴ From a manuscript description from roughly 1765 it emerges that the original *Judicirhaus* had been adorned with "stone statues" (*Steenbilleder*) that "some thirty years back", under the reign of Christian VI, had been pulled down and auctioned off. What survived until 1865 was, I shall argue, the core structure of the building.²⁵

FIG. 7.12. Andreas Vogel, painting showing the new stables in Dresden (to the left) connected with the castle (beyond the picture frame to the right) by the Long Gallery. In the middle of the wide courtyard is the "horse pool" (*Pherdeschwemme*); in the oblong *Turnierhof* one glimpses Nosseni's two bronze columns (fig. 7.23) and, high up on the wall just above them, the three arched windows of the permanent *Judicirhaus*, 1623, oil on wood, 32 × 49.5. Staatliche Kunstsammlungen, Dresden.

FIG. 7.13. Before and after Meldahl: the section of the map illustrating (1) the enclosed character of the original Tiltyard and (2) the breach through of 1865 that ruined this unity. Maps from Meldahl 1887.

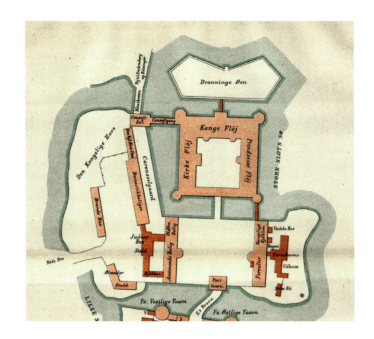

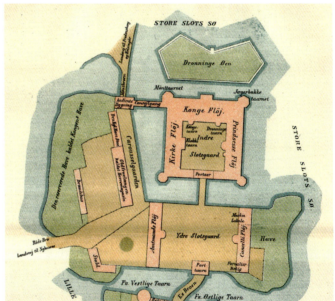

As for its original position, we have precious, but not altogether reliable information from an early bird's-eye view (fig. 1.5), which suggests that the facade of the building reached from the south-eastern corner of the Kitchen Wing's south extension across to the western

VII · THE ROYAL TILTYARD AND THE IMPERIAL PALACE OF ROME   135

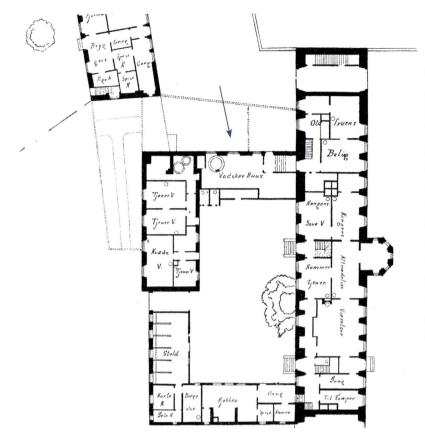

FIG. 7.14. Plan from 1862 showing the buildings originally situated in the now open space between the south end of the Kitchen Wing and the western facade of the House of the Master of the Castle. The remnants of what (it is here argued) was the *Judicirhaus* is called *Vadskerhuus* ("Laundry House"). The added arrow illustrates how the three windows of this building were positioned so that they faced the precise symmetry axis of the Tiltyard. From Beckett 1918, fig. 4.

facade of the House of the Master of the Castle, but it is unclear where precisely the linkage was.

However, the location of this linkage emerges clearly from some neglected visual evidence. First, there is a detailed ground plan from 1862, which outlines the dimensions and position of the building pulled down three years later (fig. 7.14). The plan shows that a doorway still in existence in the western facade of the so-called "House of the Master of the Castle" (*Slotsherrens Hus*) originally gave access to a hallway with a staircase leading up some five steps to an upper level, the floor of which would roughly have been about 2 metres above ground level. This elevated chamber originally had three rather tall windows and (much as in Dresden, cf. fig. 7.12), and, surely not by coincidence, the middle of

136   VII · THE ROYAL TILTYARD AND THE IMPERIAL PALACE OF ROME

FIG. 7.15. Jørgen Roed, *Karruselgården ved Frederiksborg Slot*, 1835, oil on canvas, 79 × 94. The Museum of National History at Frederiksborg.

these was intersected by the central, north-south axis of the Tiltyard.

This position and orientation by no means suggest that the original function of this edifice was that of a Laundry House (as it later became). By contrast, they evoke its original function as a *Judicirhaus*.

As for the appearance of this structure, it has hitherto been assumed that the only surviving visual record is a painting by Jørgen Roed from 1835 (fig. 7.15), which shows three rather tall stone cross windows, on the

VII · THE ROYAL TILTYARD AND THE IMPERIAL PALACE OF ROME   137

present reading probably part of what was once the judges' elevated spectator box. In any case, the facade of the surviving core structure joined the west facade of the so-called House of the Master of the Castle at right angles, just as it is shown on the plans (fig. 1.5; 7.14). At its top, it had a frieze similar to what is seen on the facade of the once richly decorated Stables (cf. fig. 7.20). As for its rear, a watercolour by Heinrich Gustav Ferdinand Holm from c.1852 (fig. 7.16), previously overlooked in this context, shows that its roof sloped

FIG. 7.16. Heinrich Gustav Ferdinand Holm, watercolour showing (right) the western rear of the Master of the Castle's House and, adjoining the latter at a right angle, the timbered rear side of the *Judicirhaus* with its roof gently sloping downwards, c.1852, 22 × 28.5. The Museum of National History at Frederiksborg.

FIG. 7.17. Photo of the *Judicirhaus* at Frederiksborg, c.1850. Antikvarisk-Topografisk Arkiv, The National Museum of Denmark.

gently backwards, again similar to what was the case at the Stables.[26]

In the Antiquarian and Topographical Archive of the Danish National Museum there are two further documents that hitherto have not been accorded the attention they deserve. One is a photograph (fig. 7.17) showing the facade of the House pulled down by Meldahl much more clearly. The photograph is a case of "reality imitating art" in as far as its chosen angle closely imitates that of Roed's popular painting (fig. 7.15), but due to the removal of a wall or wooden fence that in Roed's case partly obstructs the view, here one gets a fuller view of the *Judicirhaus*, the photo showing that beneath the three windows shown in the painting, there was, on the ground level, a corresponding, somewhat lower row of stone cross windows. This glimpse of costly, probably original window framing confirms with greater clarity what the painting shows. When this photo was taken, the small edifice with its roof line finely adjusted to match up with that of the Kitchen Building as well as with the vertical sandstone border on the facade of the House of the Master of the Castle was still essentially intact. And in its original state it clearly served well in giving the Tiltyard a visually satisfactory closure.

The second "new" document of relevance is a watercolour (fig. 7.18) by the painter Frederik Christian Lund (1826–1901) dated 6 June 1858, a year and a half before the fire. Here we still have the three lower stone cross windows, but the top three seem to have been walled in, leaving no visible trace in the wall. This change may of course be the painter's, but since he can be shown to be accurate in a similar pre-fire painting, it seems reasonable to accept his evidence as firsthand.[27] So it looks as if the painting (fig. 7.15), the photograph (fig. 7.17) and, finally, the watercolour (fig. 7.18) are evidence for considerable changes to this once splendid facade in the final decades of its existence. By the time Meldahl moved in, there may in fact have been little to preserve – except, of course, the core building and the aesthetic quality of a clearly defined, closed-in ambience.

To conclude: this lost building was obviously of a different status than that of the adjoining Kitchen. Its orientation and position indicated a different original function; so did the costly stone cross windows at a remarkably high level, which frontally intersected the central axis of the Tiltyard, circumstances easiest to

FIG. 7.18. Frederik Christian Lund, watercolour showing the Tiltyard arch at Frederiksborg. Signed and dated 6/6 1858, 36 × 40. Antikvarisk-Topografisk Arkiv, The National Museum of Denmark.

explain if what we see is in fact what until 1865 was left of the original *Judicirhaus*.

Berlin and Dresden had, in addition, a spot designated for the subsequent bathing of the horses, in Dresden in a still extant, richly ornamented *Pferdeschwemme* ("horse pool") and in Berlin in a plastered area sloping down to the banks of the Spree;[28] in Frederiksborg, where such a facility is also on record, but at a considerable distance from the Tiltyard, there was probably something similar closer by, perhaps on the banks of the lake just north of the Audience House; but this needs to be investigated further.

As for the position of the Tiltyard in relation to the residence there are further similarities. As in Berlin, where King Christian had tilted in his youth (fig. 7.8), the Frederiksborg tilting field is situated so that it faces and is visible from the castle's ceremonial wing, from the windows of the Great Hall and the windows of the Castle Chapel, as well as from the *Løngang* ("Privy Gallery") and the Audience House. In Dresden, the Long Gallery was laid out to accommodate spectators, below the arches and from the Gallery's first-floor windows. Similarly, in London, where a contemporary description from Whitehall records how the ladies of the court, among them King Christian's sister, Queen Anne (fig. 7.19), watched such a running at the ring contest from the windows of the equivalent to the Great Hall at Frederiksborg, the then Banqueting House.[29] This is probably also how it was arranged when King Christian participated in such tournaments during his visits to England in 1606 and 1614.[30]

As in Denmark (in the original layout) the tiltyards in Whitehall,[31] Dresden and Berlin were enclosed by flanking buildings, in Dresden by open loggias to one side, a closed wall to the other and gateways at either end; as for Berlin, the *Stechbahn* was closed in by the river Spree, by the castle facade and by the old cathedral, a stone balustrade further demarcating its area.[32] In Frederiksborg the Privy Gallery to the north spans the moat and connects the Royal Wing and the Audience House, and a moat and a Stable and Kitchen building ran parallel on either side of the course, which culminated at the *Judicirhaus*. Given these similarities, it is noteworthy that the facade of the Frederiksborg

FIG. 7.19. Paul van Somer, *Queen Anne of England, Scotland and Ireland with the gateway by Inigo Jones to the Palace of Oatlands in the background*, c.1617, oil on canvas, 264 × 221. Private collection.

Anne of Denmark (1574–1619) was named after her father's sister, the formidable Electress of Saxony (Keller 2010), and was the proud daughter-sister-consort of three kings. She was, like her younger brother King Christian, brought up at a court excelling in promoting the nation's fame through splendid architecture. Her father's magnificent Kronborg at Elsinore is a North European marvel, immortalised in Shakespeare's *Hamlet*. Anne herself was a dedicated patron of the arts, of theatre, music and architecture. Her promotion of Inigo Jones left as deep an impression on English architecture as her brother has left on that of his own kingdoms.

Stables originally seems to have been decorated with a stucco and paint decoration imitating a loggia (fig. 7.20) that, needless to point out, closely resembles the loggia in Dresden (fig. 7.21).

The loggia decoration was hitherto only known from a painting by Peter Christian Skovgaard (fig. 7.20), whose accuracy has been questioned. Perhaps the red-white loggia was more a *licentia poetica*, giving painterly contrast to the green of the landscape beyond.

FIG. 7.20. Peter Christian Skovgaard, *Udsigt fra Frederiksborg Slot*, 1842, oil on canvas, 140 × 150. To the right the facade of the Audience House and to its left the facade of the Stables with its stucco and painted loggia decoration. Ordrupgaard, Copenhagen.

144 · VII · THE ROYAL TILTYARD AND THE IMPERIAL PALACE OF ROME

FIG. 7.21. Carl Heinrich Jacob Fehling, *Maintenator Ringrennen* in the Dresden *Turnierhof* in 1719, 56.3 × 87.7. Staatliche Kunstsammlungen, Dresden, *Kupferstich-Kabinett*.
The grand opening of a competition between two contestants in running at the ring. Nosseni's two columns (fig. 7.12; 7.23) have therefore here been supplied with a third. To the left what looks like a temporary *Judicirhaus*, in the background the Italianate loggia of the *Turnierhof*.

Early twentieth-century scrutiny of the facade speaks in favour of the loggia, however.[33] And now, in addition, we have yet another overlooked early photograph (a companion to the one mentioned above, but looking northwards, towards the Audience House), which shows clear traces of the loggia pattern on the facade of the Stables (fig. 7.22). It seems to follow that at some point between 1835 (the date of the painting) and the early or mid-1850s (probable date of the photograph) the stucco had been stripped off, only leaving faint traces. Here as elsewhere there are, in short, clear signs that King Christian, to a high degree, had Dresden in mind when he and his architect devised the plans for his own *Turnierhof*.

VII · THE ROYAL TILTYARD AND THE IMPERIAL PALACE OF ROME   145

In tiltyards, the arch was the main adornment. There was great prestige in putting up something costly and sensational. At King Christian's coronation in 1596, the ephemeral arch was one of the major sights to behold. Reports are enthusiastic, a print showing bulging columns supporting an arch and with freestanding sculptures on their tops (fig. 7.9). For Dresden's *Turnierhof*, Giovanni Maria Nosseni, in 1601, fashioned two six-metre-tall bronze pillars in the form of Corinthian columns surmounted by obelisks between which the ring was suspended (fig. 7.23). For Frederiksborg, some ten years later, in 1614–16, Steenwinckel designed what may be termed a stone version of the temporary ceremonial arches used in Berlin and Copenhagen (fig.

FIG. 7.22. Photo of the Audience House at Frederiksborg, c.1850. Note the traces of the loggia stucco and paint on the wall to the left. Antikvarisk-Topografisk Arkiv, The National Museum of Denmark.

146 & VII · THE ROYAL TILTYARD AND THE IMPERIAL PALACE OF ROME

FIG. 7.23. Nosseni's *Turnierhof* in Dresden. The bronze columns carry the elector's coat of arms and have *obelisks* on top (the obelisks a clear allusion to the most renowned race course of them all, the *Circus Maximus* in Rome, which in its days of glory boasted two huge obelisks, one of them the largest to have survived at all). The position of the thirty-four bronze *Pilare* (of which thirteen are Nosseni's originals) that divide the field into three lanes, one to the south (right) of the pillars, one passing between them and one to the north (left) illustrate how the lost gilded obelisks at the Tiltyard at Frederiksborg might have been positioned, each of the (presumably) two rows delineating the course of the central lane, the side-lanes being demarcated by the moat to the east and the Stables to the west.

VII · THE ROYAL TILTYARD AND THE IMPERIAL PALACE OF ROME   147

7.8–9), with two lower and narrower arches flanking the central arch in which the ring would hang suspended from an intricately fashioned cast iron grill by Caspar Fincke; as on Nosseni's columns, the holes for hanging the ring are still clearly visible.

Also in Frederiksborg we learn of obelisks, in this case gilded,[34] but their function and position are uncertain. It seems a fair guess that they were intended as markers dividing the central lane from those framing it on either side (roughly like the solution adopted in Dresden, where a good dozen of Nosseni's original so-called *Pilare* have survived, fig. 7.23). In any case Steenwinckel's triple archway, which a fellow architect[35] – to Thurah's fury[36] – dismantled in the mid-1730s and replaced with the present unadorned but otherwise roughly similar structure (fig. 7.24), must have been a visual marvel, richly adorned with four coats of arms and thirteen partly gilded statues, all set up with characteristic Steenwinckel symmetry. On the ground level, there were, according to the description from 1646, two times two pairs of statues (fig. 7.25). The description seems to start with what was visible from the south, with *Ceres & Bacchus* to the right and *Diana & Apollo* to the left whereas *Pallas* (i.e. *Minerva*)[37] *& Mars* and *Venus & Hercules* stood facing north. On top of the central arch *Neptune* stood supreme, framed on either side by his royal colleagues on Mount Olympus and in Hades, *Jupiter & Juno* and *Pluto & Proserpina*.[38] The emphasis on *Neptune*, who in *singular* majesty dominates the ensemble, may at first surprise.[39] Along with this top position, the sea-gods in the pediment reliefs of the side arches stress his prominence. The arch is, as it were, his.

But, one may ask, why this emphasis? A repetition of de Vries' fountain imagery would be strangely

FIG. 7.24. Steenwinckel's sadly reduced running at the ring arch at Frederiksborg (probably designed by one Didrick Gercken) rests on the same foundations as its predecessor, but lacks the original statues. All that remains *in situ* is Caspar Fincke's gilded iron grill; the sea-god thematic of the semi-circular reliefs in the side arches suggests that they are either original or copies of the originals. Drawing from c.1914. The Danish National Art Library.

FIG. 7.25. Digital reconstruction by Kirsten Marie Kragelund of the arch as it may have looked originally. The position of the putti with the coats of arms, of the five top statues and of the four ground-level statues follow the indications of a description from 1646, but the visual detail is, in the main, purely conjectural.

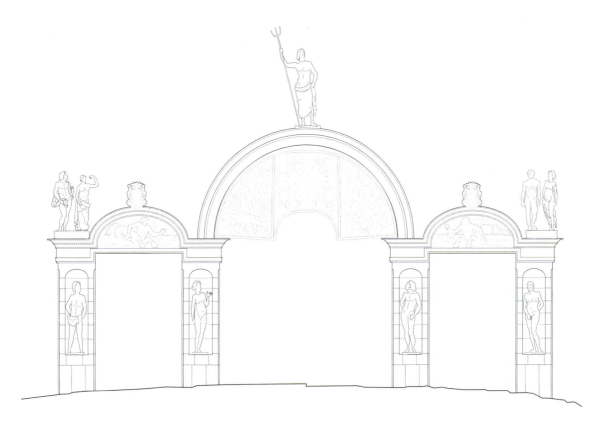

VII · THE ROYAL TILTYARD AND THE IMPERIAL PALACE OF ROME

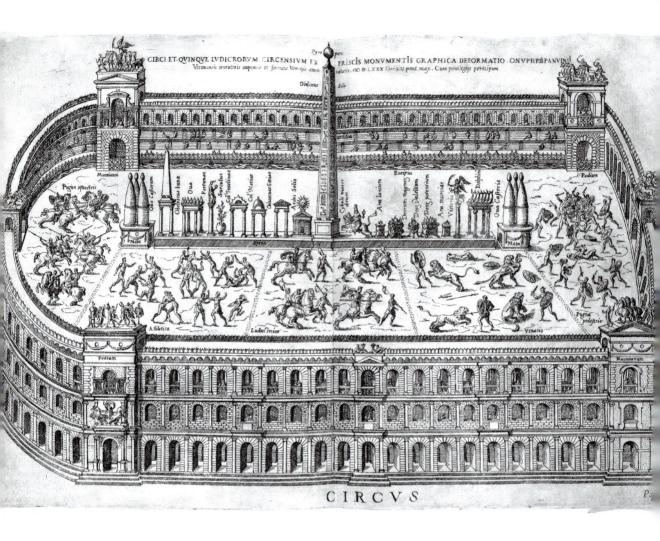

pointless. Resen's reference to the "Troy Game" provides the clue. His use of this technical term suggests that he (or his informant) knew about the ambitions surrounding this project. In ancient Rome, the so-called *lusus Troiae* (Troy Game) was celebrated in the *Circus Maximus*;[40] reputedly instituted by the legendary founder of Rome, Aeneas from Troy, these games brought together youths of the highest nobility, with strong emphasis on the eminence of the contestants. Winners in contests won prizes (just as in the runnings at the ring). The location was important; the race

FIG. 7.26. The *Circus Maximus* as conjecturally restored by Onofrio Panvinio in c.1580 in his *De ludis circensibus*, Venice 1600. The copy at the Royal Danish Library was acquired in 1602 by the noble Sigvard (Sivert) Grubbe (1566–1636), a courtier of Christian IV.

course for such *lusus* ran along the valley right beneath the Imperial Palace on the Palatine.

These imperial associations that create a flattering parallel between the iconic palace of the Roman Caesars and King Christian's castle are further underlined by the dominant role of Neptune, high on top of the central gateway. Neptune, the divine horse tamer, was in fact in his role as Consus the patron god of Rome's *Circus Maximus*,[41] a circumstance no doubt influencing Steenwinckel and his humanist advisors in choosing to dedicate King Christian's Tiltyard to Neptune himself.

Here as in Dresden, moreover, the use of obelisks, in Dresden in bronze, in Denmark gilded, as part of the decorative programme is unmistakable in pointing back to the legendary Roman circuses, at the Vatican, at the *Circus Maximus* and at the Circus of Maxentius. The recent campaigns of Pope Sixtus v in re-erecting Rome's obelisks had of course created renewed awareness of the old links between obelisks and hippodromes.[42]

Like its ancient counterpart (as it had famously been reconstructed by Onofrio Panvinio in 1580 (fig. 7.26)), this modern *Circus Maximus* was at one end rounded off with an arch, in this case more poetic than triumphal, the exuberant design of which Steenwinckel borrowed from a treatise on architecture by Wendel Dietterlin from 1598 (fig. 7.27) that was in his brother's and later his own possession (and is now preserved at the Royal Danish Library).[43] As was typical in the period's ephemeral "architecture", set up to mark the ceremonial entry of a monarch, the arch is crowned by a whole array of interacting mythological figures, the theme for this particular assembly taken from the episode in Ovid's *Metamorphoses* where Minerva, the goddess of wisdom and the arts, visits the Muses on Helicon (also

FIG. 7.27. Wendel Dietterlin, *Architectura*, Nürnberg 1598, book 4, *Corinthia*, fig. 160. The copy here reproduced bears the autograph owners' marks of the two brothers Steenwinckel. The Royal Danish Library.

called Mount Parnassus); she inspects the Hippocrene fountain that inspires poetry and, on their invitation, "takes a seat in the grove's light shadow" to listen to their song (fig. 7.28). Dietterlin's and after him Steenwinckel's Ovidian tableau (fig. 7.29) ultimately draws upon the iconographical tradition of the sixteenth-century illustrated editions of Ovid's *Metamorphoses*, from Mainz 1545, Venice 1553 and Lyon (from 1557 repeatedly up to 1609).[44] This Ovidian thematic of the arch was, probably during a later reign, developed further in the lake to the north of the castle, where a monumental fountain was set up depicting a stag being attacked by dogs. Clearly, this was Diana taking her revenge on Actaeon in the very forests that the castle's sculptures would declare belonged to her (cf. fig. 3.18; 4.15).[45]

But, returning to the Audience House, there are, above this almost life-size Ovidian *tableau*, with *Minerva* listening and the *Muses* playing the musical instruments of the time, further such instruments put on display as the *spolia* of a peace-time triumph. Within the cartouche, moreover, a whole array of trumpets frames the central relief, these instruments being the silent echoes of the vibrant musical culture of the Danish court, where, during King Christian's reign, it was possible to hear performers and composers such as Heinrich Schütz, Mogens Pedersen, William Brade and John Dowland. Like the court painters, these musicians were treasured elements of the cultural assets that the Danish court not only applauded and supported, but also used to boost its prestige in relation to the related courts at Dresden, Gottorp, Mecklenburg, Berlin, Wolfenbüttel and, of course, London.[46] Like the court of his sister, Queen Anne, King Christian's was indeed demonstrative in cultivating the music and the Muses, even to the point of having them depicted on the facade

of his Audience House. It therefore seems suggestive that this unusual group of sculptures once had a notable life-size parallel in the London gardens of Queen Anne, herself a great music lover. There, on the banks of the Thames behind her residence at Somerset House, she let the French garden engineer Salomon de Caus (c.1576–1626) fashion a colossal garden fountain in the form of Mount Parnassus on top of which stood a golden Pegasus; in a grotto (garden grottoes being a *must* in Italian, French and now also English gardens) one saw *Apollo,* and on the mountain's slopes the *Muses* playing their modern-style instruments, just as in Frederiks-

FIG. 7.28. The statue groups of the Audience House with Minerva and the Muses at Helicon and, in the central field, Mars and Venus, 1614–15. The Muses are playing flute, lute, viol, viola da gamba and harp.

FIG. 7.29. Minerva and the Muses at Helicon and, in the central field, Mars and Venus. Drawing of the south facade of the Audience House (fig. 7.28) by Charles Christensen and Asger Jeppesen, 1917. Danish National Art Library.

borg. De Caus started working for Queen Anne in 1609 and by 1613 the huge *Parnassus* is known to have been in place in what, in a Nordic context, was probably the most avant-garde mannerist garden of the period. As Roy Strong observes, "in permanent form" the fountain expresses "an iconographic programme typical of Anne of Denmark"[47] – as, indeed, of her brother, who no doubt saw this hydraulic marvel when, during his surprise visit in July 1614, he stayed with his sister in Somerset or, as it was then flatteringly called, Denmark House (fig. 7.30). There, one "night in the garden, by the king of Denmark's device and charge, and by his

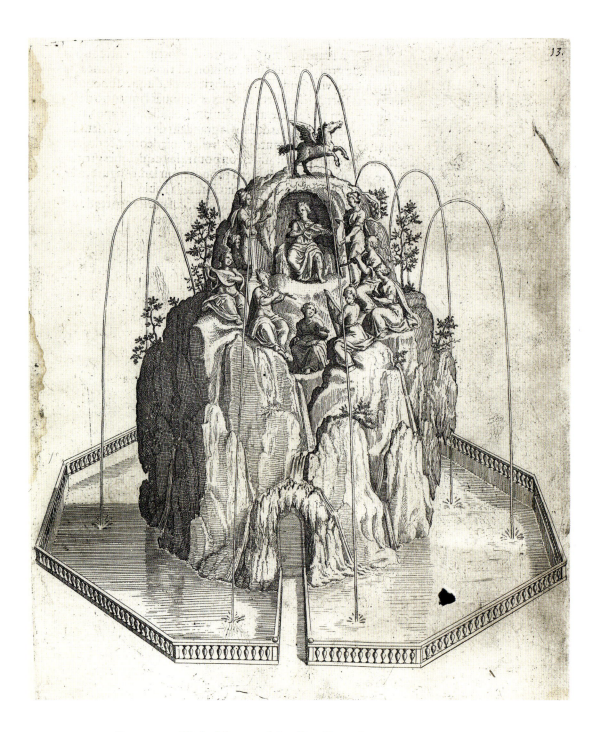

FIG. 7.30. Parnassus with the Muses and Apollo, a Fountain roughly similar to the one set up by de Caus in the garden of Queen Anne at Somerset House in London. From Salomon de Caus, *Les Raisons des Forces Mouvantes,* vol. II, Paris 1615, tab. xiii.

owne men, there were performed most excellent and ingenious fireworks."[48] Later, when commissioning a ceremonial gateway for his Audience House from Steenwinckel (work began that same summer),[49] the motif of the life-size Muses giving a concert, as in his music-loving sister's garden, may well be an echo of what he saw on his second visit to London.

Be this as it may, the imagery chosen certainly has other personal associations. Right in the middle of the scene with the Muses, Steenwinckel placed a superimposed relief (thus leaving no space for two of the nine Muses), its cartouche relief illustrating a mythological

FIG. 7.31. Laurens Steenwinckel and workshop, *Mars and Venus* (detail from fig. 7.29).

VII · THE ROYAL TILTYARD AND THE IMPERIAL PALACE OF ROME   157

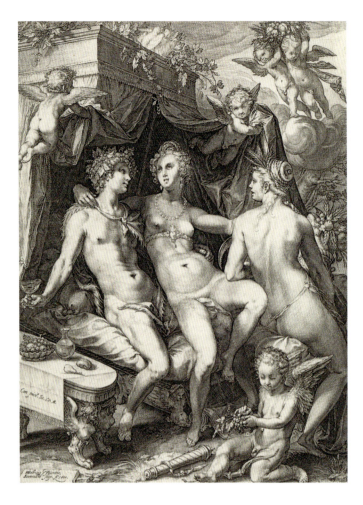

FIG. 7.32. Jan Saenredam after Hubert Goltzius, *Bacchus, Venus and Ceres,* 1600, 43.1 × 31.6. Rijksmuseum, Amsterdam.

episode with the war god Mars finding loving comfort in the arms of the goddess of love (fig. 7.31), an erotic theme right out of the Italian-style madrigals so beloved by the court of Christian IV (and, as it has been plausibly suggested, also an allusion to the king's affair with his long-lasting *maitresse en titre*, Kirsten Munk). As a model for this relief, the sharp-eyed Meir Stein spotted a print by Hubert Goltzius (1528–83) representing Bacchus, Venus and Ceres (fig. 7.32).[50] The parallels between the print and the relief are numerous, both with respect to the position of the two lovers,

FIG. 7.33. Bartolomeo Bagnacavallo, *Mars and Cupid*, c.1530. Staatliche Graphische Sammlung, Munich.

who at Frederiksborg are, of course, less undressed, but Venus' thigh still rests across his – and then there is the canopied bed, the Cupids, the table and the presence of Ceres. However, like Goltzius, Steenwinckel also seems to have taken a close look at a print (fig. 7.33) by Bartolommeo Bagnacavallo (1484–1542), this time only with Mars and Venus. The splendid vase, the God's discarded shield and the playful Cupid with his arrow may well come from there – or, of course, from inventive minds trained in imagining the décor of such celestial abodes.

VII · THE ROYAL TILTYARD AND THE IMPERIAL PALACE OF ROME   159

FIG. 8.1. Reinhold Timm, *Musicians at the court of Christian IV*, c.1621–25, oil on canvas, 207 × 113.5. The Danish Music Museum, Copenhagen – Musikhistorisk Museum & The Carl Claudius Collection. At the heigth of his power, Christian IV employed about 140 musicians and singers. The English harpist Darby Scott (first from the left), who played Irish harp, had been hired in 1621; Thomas Simpson, who sits next to him, left the court in 1625.

ENVOI

Palatial Settings for a "Ceremonial Court"

Musical instruments are a recurrent theme in Frederiksborg's imagery. Music to praise the Lord crowns the gateway to the Royal Chapel (fig. 4.9) and joined by poetry's *Pegasus* such instruments are also on show in the pediment above the entrance to the stair turret of the Great Hall (fig. 8.2). Across the moat, at the gateway of the Audience House, this joyful aspect of court life also manifests itself there abundantly (fig. 7.28).

In permanent form, this iconography evokes music that accompanied numerous court functions, be it in the Chapel, with its organ, in the Great Hall, with its musicians' balcony, or from atop the Terrace at the arrival of princes or envoys. Such festive rituals are part of what has rightly been defined as a new devel-

FIG. 8.2. Pediment of the entrance gate to the stair turret giving access to the Great Hall at Frederiksborg.

FIG. 8.3. Allegorical figures (*Mercury playing for Argus* and *Venus and Amor*) on the front of the organ built by Essias Compenius in 1610. The organ, which today can be seen and heard in the Chapel, was originally placed in the Great Hall, not for church use, but for dance music. The Museum of National History at Frederiksborg.

opment in Danish court life, marking the transition from the "patriarchal court" of the king's grandfather to the increasingly ceremonial organisation of life and interaction in the courts of Frederik II and, above all, Christian IV.[1] Emphasis on hierarchy, on display and magnificence and on the rich and dignified setting for arrivals, processions, church functions, dances and concerts (fig. 8.3), hunts and jousting festivities are, it has here been argued, the modern components of court life that King Christian's new castle was intended to provide with a dauntingly impressive, but also facilitating architectural frame. What the king had seen, at its most expansively ceremonial and fullest flowering at Theobalds and at the courts of his cousins and in-laws in Dresden and Berlin,[2] was here given the solid shape of brick, bronze and sandstone and decked out with silver and gilding. The resulting frame, with its splendid and, at the same time, clearly defined routes of ceremonial access as well as spaces of interaction is, to an unprecedented degree in Denmark, populated by

FIG. 8.4. The Anointment of Christian VI in 1731. The procession crosses the Courtyard of Frederiksborg. Guache by Johann Jacob Bruun, c.1737, 24.3 × 20.1. The Museum of National History at Frederiksborg. Note the spectators atop the Terrace and on the Marble Gallery.

sculptures, often almost life-size, that allow ancestry and Protestantism, but first and foremost the august realm of classical history and myth to play a visible, almost tangible, role in the castle's stage-like court life.

Given these qualities it seems logical that the absolutist successors of Christian IV chose Frederiksborg as the setting for the solemn anointment festivities marking the beginning of each new reign.[3] Until the end of Danish Absolutism in 1849, every new monarch's accession was celebrated with a procession that

FIG. 8.5. The last of the Absolutist anointments: Johan Vilhelm Gertner, *The procession of King Christian VIII leaves the Chapel at Frederiksborg*, 1851, oil on canvas, 29.2 × 26.6. The Royal Danish Collection, Rosenborg.

FIG. 8.6. Pieter Isaacsz, *Allegory on Øresund* (with Kronborg in the background). Neptune and Cybele stand united and trade is blossoming, 1622, oil on canvas, 259 × 307. The National Gallery of Denmark (in deposit at Kronborg).

started in the Audience House, the new king then traversing the Marble Gallery where he, standing in the gallery's centre, would for the first time receive the acclamation of the assembly of dignitaries gathering in the castle courtyard (Danish Absolutism would allow no coronation, since kings owed no mortal being but only God their high position on earth).

From the Gallery the procession then continued down the queen's staircase, and across the courtyard (fig. 8.4–5) finally to enter the Chapel, where the bishops of the Realms would anoint the new monarch. For such pageantry Frederiksborg's exuberance of sculpture and its dazzling architectural frame provided an ideal setting – a setting that even today preserves an, admittedly fragmentary, but still unusually evocative visual echo of a great ceremonial past.

In words borrowed from Shakespeare's Danish play: *Here* "is the beauteous Majesty of Denmark" (*Hamlet*, Act IV, sc. 5).

Notes

CHAPTER I

1. The main contemporary witnesses are Berg 1646 and Resen c.1688 (translation of vol. II from Latin into Danish by Hertig 1994); Thurah 1749, 3–62 and Rasbech 1832 discuss later developments; the descriptions by Wolf 1654 and by Gerner c.1680 are based upon Berg 1646 and add nothing new. Jessen c.1765 closely follows Thurah but has some additional evidence: ch. VII, n. 23 and 25; contemporary travel accounts (surveyed in Ilsøe 1963 and 2015) by Charles de Lespine (c.1620), Prince Christian of Anhalt-Bernburg (1623), Johann von Hoverbeck (1639), François Blondel (1653), Raimondo Montecuccoli (1654), Carl Gustav Heräus (1694) and la Combe de Vrigny (c.1700) are quoted in ch. II, n. 6; ch. III, n. 4; n. 35; ch. IV, n. 7; ch. V, n. 23; ch. VI, n. 2 and ch. VII, n. 13.
2. Rasbech 1832, 98: "Det er forresten mærkeligt ved dette Slot, at man intetsteds i Landet finder en større Samling af Figurer og antique Statuer, tjenende til Prydelse for nogen enkelt Bygning i Særdeleshed, end netop her…"
3. On the architecture of Christian IV, Andersen, Nyborg & Vedsø 2010, 23–31 gives an excellent, updated survey; in languages other than Danish, check Skovgaard 1973, Roding 1991 and Christianson 2009.
4. The description is at the beginning of the third canto of Erasmus Laetus' *Margaretica*, Frankfurt am Main 1573: Skovgaard-Petersen 1988, 21–22.
5. The king's learned chancellor Cristen Friis (1581–1639) was involved in formulating a programme for the king's series of victory tapestries: Degn 1988, 18–20. Such men were doubtless also active when it came to Frederiksborg's sculptural programme.

CHAPTER II

1. Impact of Vredeman de Vries: Bartetzky 2005 and Johannsen 2005, both with bibliography; of Wendel Dietterlin: Neumann 2011, 70–74 and Ottenheym 2011, 321–22 with this book's fig. 7.27; on the king and the arts, see Heiberg 2007 and Olden Jørgensen 2007 (both with bibliography). The fountain in Vries' *oeuvre*: Scholten 1998, 218–27; on the original fountain, see Wanscher 1937, 92–93; Larsson 1967, 67–73; Kommer 2000, 283–88; Christensen 2006, 155–72 (all convincingly arguing for a lower, more restrained pedestal).
2. On their triumphant progress through London in 1606 the kings Christian and James paused before a huge arch, from which they were addressed in Latin, first by *London*, then by *Neptune*: Dyson 1606, 22–23; cf. the summary in a report from 7 August 1606 quoted in the Cecil *Calendar* 1606; a slogan

launched during the visit was "Seamen kingdomes, now againe united": Ford 1606, unpag.
3   Berg 1646, unpag. reports that Adriaen de Vries' *Mercury* held the cipher of Christian IV; on the original, now in Sweden, it has been removed, but it has been included in the restored version.
4   "Dominium": Heiberg 2017, 355; the four dragons on top of the Copenhagen Exchange likewise symbolise Danish outreach, across the oceans, to all four corners of the world: Roding 2010, 243–44.
5   Berg 1646, unpag. reports that the statues stood "auff Tuscanischen Seulen, nach Lebens grösse, in weissen Quartersteinen gehawen und vergüldet"; the figure to the right ("zur Rechten"), which I here take to be heraldic right, i.e. to the left of the person approaching the castle, was *Julius Caesar* and to the right *Alexander the Great*; by the mid-eighteenth century the columns and statues were gone: Thurah 1749, 11; they were cut anew by N. Chr. Petersen in 1909–10 (Weilbach 1923, 98), but wrongly repositioned: the *Caesar* went where *Alexander* should have been and *vice versa*.
6   Much of the castle's sculpture was originally gilded, as witnessed i.a. by Blondel 1653, unpag., "et peut on rien voir de plus beau/ que cette structure de brique:/ le marbre & l'or de tous costés/ iettent de si vives clartés/"; for further evidence for gilding, see la Combe de Vrigny 1706, 142 ("cuivre doré" on the facade of the Chapel Wing) and ch. III, n. 35; ch. V, n. 23; ch. VI, n. 2; ch. VII, n. 34 and 38. Silver was also much in evidence, as witnessed by Charles de Lespine in c.1620: Lachère 1935, 120; Beckett 1914, 112 summarises what could still be seen of gilding and of colouring of the pediments in his own day.
7   Rosenthal 1971, 204–28.

CHAPTER III

1   Beckett 1914, 39–40; 69–70 summarises the agreement between the king and Steenwinckel concerning the new Terrace; Wanscher 1937, 56; 98 sees the whole south facade as original, its rear-side loggia being added in 1619. Archaeology disproves this view: Beckett 1914, 39; Steenberg 1950, 51; as shown by Steffen Heiberg, so does the portrait from c.1615 of young Frederik III by Pieter Isaacsz (fig. 3.2): Mellbye-Hansen 1988, 3–4.
2   On the Castle Chapel, the contributions by Johannsen 1970, 1974 and those by the same scholar reprinted in Andersen, Nyborg & Vedsø 2010 are fundamental.
3   Beckett 1914, 39.
4   "Gothic" asymmetry (for instance in the position of the Chapel tower and unequal width of the side wings): Lorenzen 1945, 463–65; Bramsen 1982, 48–49; Smith 2006, 270–73; similarly Lyngby & Skougaard 2009, 25; by contemporaries, this aspect came increasingly to be seen as an aesthetic defect: Ilsøe 1965, 10 (quoting a travel account from 1639 seeing the castle as built in a German style (as opposed to Italian), the so-called German style already then considered unfashionable); similarly Heräus 1694, 567: the castle was beautiful, but "l'architecture n'en est de plus regulière ny moderne, d'ou vient que du loin il paroissent quatre tours mal arrangées."
5   "The Baroque to Denmark": thus my partner Mogens Nykjær (private conversation); similarly, Neumann 2011, 69–70, who rightly foregrounds formal similarities with the baroque Palais Richelieu (1629) in Paris. In 1602, the young king wanted all his father's buildings on the three islands pulled down, one after another: Beckett 1914, 33–34. Steenberg 1950, 26–27 sees topographical reasons for abandoning this plan after c.1620. As Steffen Heiberg informs me, economy was hardly the problem. I am indebted to the fellow members of the Selskab for Dansk Kulturhistorie (meeting in May 2016) for reminding me that while the S-bridge may

well be a second-best, it also provides a typically mannerist change of focus.

6 Beckett 1914, 41–50; Skovgaard 1973, 45–51; Skovgaard 2006, 67; the original prototype for such an entrance is of course Philibert de l'Orme's Castle of Anet (1552); the fame of du Cerceau: Guillaume, Fuhring & Auclair 2010 (with bibliography).

7 Steenwinckel visiting France: Nørregaard-Nielsen 1980, 36; but the evidence is, at best, indirect; in any case, chronology speaks against seeing him as the author of the new masterplan. Copies of du Cerceau probably in the library of Christian IV: Skovgaard 1973, 49. De Bray's *Architectura moderna* (1631) shows that the circle around de Keyser knew Steenwinckel well: Ottenheym 2011, 316–17.

8 Theobalds: Stein 1987, 82–89. Unaware of Stein's argument, Randsborg 2004, 85 mentions Theobalds as a possible inspiration for the loggias at Frederiksborg but goes no further. Neumann 2011, 73–74 rightly points to similarities with the English use of facade loggias, for instance at Cecil's Hatfield from 1607 (not seen by Christian), but does not mention Theobalds.

9 "welches vor eines der schönsten Häuser in Engellandt gehalten würdt, wie es dann auch in wa(h)rheit ist", Rathgeben 1603, 32 (= Rye 1865, 44–45); annotation in the copy of Rathgeben in the Royal Danish Library (Geog. 954, 4°, 41235, cf. Wanscher 1937, 53) shows it was given by King Christian to one Hennigh Waldorff in 1606, before or after the journey (with thanks to Marianne Alenius for help with deciphering); "expansive symmetry": Summerson 1993, 69; Theobalds' impact on British architecture: Dunlop 1962, 166–79; Airs 2002; Cole 2017, 71–72; 107–8.

10 Andrews 1993, 135 and Summerson 1959, 116 (quoting a report from 1650). At https://library.thehumanjourney.net/77/1/BROXCP07.pdf one can access a 2008 Oxford Archaeological report on the surviving ruins and the park (with thanks to Dr Ann Benson for the reference and to the chairman and members of the Enfield Archaeological Society for a stimulating tour through the area in January 2017).

11 Summerson 1959, pl. xxii–xxxiii.

12 Blunt 1999, 91–92.

13 The total of five loggias at Theobalds is unique in the architecture of the period: Henderson 1995, 118; Airs 2002, 6–7.

14 "Gallery": Summerson 1959, 110; 118 with a tentative reconstruction in pl. xxxii b.

15 For Theobalds' succession of courtyards, Sutton 2004, 30–47 and Cole 2017 offer a detailed and nuanced reading (with ample bibliography). Theobalds' gallery was delivered by the Flemish sculptor Hendrik van Paesschen (or van Passe) in 1569–70: Summerson 1959, 110; Paesschen had worked first at the Antwerp Town Hall, then at London's Royal Exchange (Ottenheym & De Jonge 2007, 233), where he was contracted by Cecil also to deliver the new sandstone facade for Theobalds. The workshop of Hendrick de Keyser in Amsterdam delivered sculptures, reliefs, columns and arches for the Gallery at Frederiksborg in 1619–21: Chs. IV–VI. The impact of the Theobalds gallery on that of Frederiksborg: Cole 2017, 107.

16 Floris and prefab loggias: Ottenheym 2013.

17 Theobalds' walkway: Cole 2017, 83.

18 Crowds in their hundreds (if not more) followed the royal procession all the way from London to Theobalds: Roberts 1606a, unpag. = Nichols 1828, vol. II, 62. The interest in the visit is amply confirmed by the number of pamphlets, poems and sermons published during King Christian's stay and after his departure; Neville Davis 1992 and Shapiro 2015, 398–402 survey contemporary sources concerning the visit and the theatricals at Theobalds. The three boys standing in "hollows" adorned with cloth: mss diary (24 July 1606) in the Royal Danish Library, *NKS* 364c, 24 July 1606 (a reference I owe Dr Cay Dollerup).

19 Sutton 2004, 171–83 surveys and discusses the elaborate welcome ceremonies in detail; however, Heaton 2010, 125–62 shows that some of the manuscript evidence quoted refers to an altogether

different ceremony. The total costs for the four days at Theobalds amounted to £ 1180: Cecil *Calendar* 16 August 1606 (a day-labourer earned about £10 a year, so expenditure for four days amounted to a staggering equivalent of 118 annual wages).
20 Theatricals at Theobalds: Sutton 2004, 169–94 and Shapiro 2015, 289–317 (with further bibliography).
21 Shapiro 2015, 306–7 argues convincingly that Harington is an unreliable witness, his report concerning the scandalous Queen of Sheba masque almost "too good to be true"; similarly, Wiggins & Richardson 2015, 309 (perhaps "a satirical fiction"). I am indebted to Bent Holm for pointing out that there was a masque and that female actors were the norm: this aspect of Harington's report seems rooted in fact.
22 Much special pleading concerning all involved, for instance when Dyson 1606, 8 agrees that Denmark had a reputation for "free-hearted intertainment, or to(o) great delight in drinke", but that the king's entourage were so abstemious that they "exceeded the sevearest Italian." Similarly, it was for an anti-royalist writing after the execution of Charles I James, not Christian, who was carried drunk to bed at Theobalds: Peyton 1652, 63–64.
23 Howes 1615, 886 = Nichols 1828, vol. II, 87.
24 The theatrical display in Henry VII's Chapel: Shapiro 2015, 312–13.
25 Howes 1615, 886 = Nichols 1828, vol. II, 87.
26 Work on the Frederiksborg Chapel started in September 1606: Johannsen 1970, 1689; visual evidence for the Chapel's suddenly increased height: fig. 3.3–4; "Tudoresque": Wanscher 1937, 52.
27 Roberts 1606b, unpag. = Nichols 1828, vol. II, 81; contra, the letter writer Dudley Carleton (ed. Lee, 1972, 87): "the king … was not observed much to admire anything he saw, though he was curious to see much"; but while Roberts clearly followed events closely, Carleton seems more distant and with no acknowledgement of linguistic barriers: the common language of hosts and guest would have been Latin, in which James was more fluent than Christian. A person as visually aware and "curious" as King Christian would probably have taken in much more than he said.
28 "alleeneste for at besee Tøyhuset, hvoraf saa stor Rye og Rygte gik", Slange 1749, 121.
29 Du Cerceau and Cecil House: Husselby & Henderson 2002, 170; Henderson 2005, 10 (ground plan in colour).
30 Cecil was probably happy to be relieved of the costly and no longer essential residence; for him the exchange was in fact profitable: Dunlop 1962, 178; Henderson 2006, 403; Heaton 2010, 178–79 and Cole 2017, 105; contra, but unconvincingly, Sutton 2004, 196–208.
31 In Danish, she is Anna, but for convenience I follow modern English usage; Theobalds' transfer to "Bel-Anna" (22 May 1607) is celebrated in the masque by Ben Jonson quoted by Nichols 1828, vol. II, 128–31 at 130.
32 Laurids Jacobsen Hindsholm, in 1648: "(the king had sometimes) selff giffvet dennem (sc. the craftsmen) Affritzning oc Model, med egen Haand giort, til efterretning" (quoted from Schepelern 1973, 30); for more than a century, the debate concerning the king's involvement in his building projects has moved from implausible extremes of total involvement, the king himself being the chief architect, to the equally implausible alternative of total disinvolvement. A compromise, acknowledging his dedication and leaving room for proper builders, is what seems to be called for: Schepelern 1973, 32–33.
33 In Denmark, King Frederik II's *Lundehave* (1587) outside Elsinore had an early, but not quite classical, forerunner: Beckett 1914, 61. In Sweden, King Johan III's wildly pioneering and, sadly, lost *Svartsjö* (1590s) and the courtyard of his Trekroner palace at Stockholm had classical loggias. At Frederiksborg it was only at this late stage that classical elements – as transmitted by Wendel Dietterlin – were adapted: Neumann 2011, 70–74.
34 Pontoppidan 1764, 306 saw the names of these "heathen divinities" as irrelevant ("nogle hedenske Diviniteter, som icke ere værd at opregne"), but Berg 1646, unpag. and Thurah 1749, 14 give

complete lists: from the gateway eastwards stood NEPTUNE, AMPHITRITE, HERCULES, OMPHALE, PHOEBUS and LUNA; from the gateway westwards JUPITER, JUNO, MARS, VENUS, HIPPOMENES and ATALANTA; Weilbach 1923, 100 and Mellbye-Hansen 1988, unpag. observe that *Omphale* has been replaced by a *Minerva*, probably during a later restoration campaign.

35 Terrace statues gilded: thus a visitor in 1623 (= Krause 1858, 101); for the otherwise unrecorded visit at Nonsuch, see the mss. diary (3–4 August 1606) quoted n. 30. Nonsuch ("Nunttis") he describes as a *megitt statelig slot, och fick Mad der thill Middag och der Uden paa skønne historier giort aff Gips och forgyllt*, "a very imposing palace and we had lunch there, and on the outside there were handsome tales done in gypsum and gilded."

36 Mellbye-Hansen 1988, unpag. doubts the identification with Atalanta and Hippomenes, finding the subject too esoteric. But the motif was well known from Ovid (*Metamorphoses* 10.560–710) and enjoyed great popularity in the Renaissance and later: Reid 1993, vol. I, 237–40 and Dewes 2011 and Huber-Rebenich et al. 2014, B 391–98 (reproductions in illustrated editions from the fifteenth century onwards). No reason, therefore, to doubt what Berg and Thurah report: Kragelund 2006, 46; the suggested motivation for the group's position is accepted by Lyngby 2017, 158.

37 Weilbach 1923, 102 observes that the statue now to be seen is a *Bacchus* (with a bunch of grapes in hand) that replaces an original *Hippomenes*; interestingly, an attempt seems to have been made to give his activity a semblance of the original's. Unesco World Heritage: Baagøe 2015.

CHAPTER IV

1 The disturbing asymmetry of the original facade: Rasbech 1832, 99; Weilbach 1923, 108; Steenberg 1950, 29 fig. 6; Johannsen 1970, 1694–96 and Skovgaard 1973, 51; the ground plan and elevation in Thurah 1749, pl. vi and x (fig. 4.3) show that the centrality and monumentality of the museum's present-day main entrance and central *piano nobile* window is a nineteenth-century alteration introduced by Meldahl: fig. 4.4. Meldahl's drawings for this new monumental entrance are held in the Danish National Art Library 258, mappe 6, 50553.

2 Such ideals spread slowly: Bedoire 2001 and Noldus 2004, 19–46 examine how they gradually came to be accepted by the Swedish nobility; from his master Hendrick de Keyser, Steenwinckel would around 1610 have picked up similar lessons; and so would King Christian, from his visit to Theobalds (ch. III).

3 Traces of a wooden balcony: Beckett 1914, 255; Steenberg 1950, 29. The museum's otherwise excellent video on the castle's building history (cf. ch. VII, n. 24) shows the facade from 1606 as having had a monumental central gateway, but this is pure anachronistic fantasy.

4 Beckett 1914, 125 points to similarities with the castle in Ancy-le-Franc as it was published by du Cerceau (facade with the horizontal pattern: arch, column, niche, column, arch, etc.); Steenwinckel's use of such publications: ch. VII, n. 43. For English parallels, see Neumann 2011, 73–74 (cf. ch. III, n. 8).

5 The Italianate loggia at Güstrow (which Christian IV visited in 1595): Weingart 2006; Saxony and Denmark: Kappel & Brink 2009; on architecture in particular, see Johannsen in: Andersen, Nyborg & Vedsø 2010, 71–88.

6 The Dresden Gallery and the Vatican: Dombrowski 2007.

7 Montecuccoli 1654, 16: the castle was "bello nel di fuori e nel cortile, che ha una fonte nel mezzo, con statue di bronzo; dentro ha poco buona architettura nelle scale, ne' lumi, e negli anditi"; Heräus 1694,

567: "l'escalier (i.e. of Frederiksborg) ne repond point à la magnificence du dehors."

8 In Denmark's royal architecture, the first monumental, internal staircase is the wooden and clumsy so-called "Great Italian Staircase" at the palace of Charlottenborg in Copenhagen from the 1670s.

9 Delft a showpiece: Ottenheym & De Jonge 2007, 230. For reports on de Keyser and his workshop, see Beckett 1914, 128–29; Thorlacius-Ussing 1945, 108–10; Ottenheym, Rosenberg & Smit 2008, 118–19 (with bibliography). The oeuvre of Gerrit Lambertsen is brought "out of de Keyser's shadow" in the groundbreaking work by Ottenheym & Jonge 2013, 68–69 and Vries 2016.

10 Berg 1646, unpag. (describing the facade of the eastern wing): "über den Fenstern sind manche Felder, darein allerley Römische Geschichte, mit beygeschriebenen Namen zubeschau, von welchem die nach den innersten Platz alle mit halbgeschlagenem Golde überzogen." The surviving inscribed portraits of Danish kings from Frederiksborg's facades are – to judge from the records – not distributed according to any recognisable chronological or thematic pattern. It is a fair guess that the confusion is caused either by Meldahl (cf. ch. IV, n. 16) or by pre-fire restorers.

11 I am grateful to Dr Steffen Heiberg, who years ago pointed out Caesar under the westernmost arch of the Gallery (the original is now in the museum's *Lapidarium*); it is numbered and inscribed: "I IVLI"(i.e. "No. 1, IVLI(us Caesar)"). Caesar is followed by no. 2 Augustus, the "son of Divine Caesar" (inscribed "2 DIVI FILI(us) A(ugustus)"; no. 3 (Tiberius) is lost and has been replaced by a (mistakenly divinised) Galba, "DIV(u)S GALBA"; then follows no. IIII (Caius = Caligula) inscribed "IIII C .../ DI(vi) AVG(usti), probably originally with an added N(epos) ("grandson" (in fact great-grandson of Divus Augustus)); then comes no. 5, "V CLAVDIVS". No. 6 Nero seems lost. The original "A(ulus) VITEL(lius) ... AVGVST(us)" is now (and then?) found over the eastern window in the Terrace Building's Loggia (with thanks to the museum's curator Dr Per Seesko for help with a ladder to check the inscription); "XII DOMITIAN(us)", i.e. "Number twelve, Domitian" is now in the museum's *Lapidarium* (like the others, it is not known from where it was taken down).

12 On such series, see e.g. Stupperich 1995, 39–58; Fittschen 2015, 201–22; Beard 2014 offers a broad and incisive survey; on Meldahl's careless practice when restoring architecture, sculpture and imagery, see further ch. IV, n. 16.

13 The late Hugo Johannsen's "Regna Firmat Pietas" = Johannsen 1974, 67–140 was pioneering in applying an iconographical approach to the imagery of the Royal Chapel of Frederiksborg; for Johannsen's subsequent contributions, see ch. III, n. 2 and Andersen, Nyborg & Vedsø, 2010.

14 Reindel 2009, 38; cf. Reindel 2015, 71–86 (with bibliography).

15 Bligaard 2008, vol. II, 32–33.

16 Meldahl 1887, 61; Bligaard 2008, vol. II, 343–55 offers a circumspect survey of Meldahl's strengths (respect, when possible, for original materials); as for his weaknesses, note his dismantling of the Judicirhaus (ch. VII, n. 24), his failure to record original positions of sculpture as well as his ignoring early sources concerning Frederiksborg (cf. ch. IV, nn. 10, 12, 18 and 25).

17 Bligaard 2008, vol. II, 32 lists the numbers; for the gods and heroes until recently on exhibit, see Kragelund 2006, 307–8 n. 34.

18 Olden Jørgensen 2006, 124–25 examines a parallel case, the costly, but highly arbitrary reconstruction of the ceiling in the Great Hall, a reconstruction based exclusively on Berg 1646, while it, to its detriment, ignores the very detailed and far more accurate descriptions of the ceiling in Thurah 1749 and Rasbech 1832.

19 Plans for the ongoing restoration of Frederiksborg are at the point of writing still in the making.

20 Friis 1877, 31 publishes Sweys' contract for the Gallery from 1621.

21 Stein 1972, 284–93 (re-edited in Danish in Stein 1987, 109–21) does not discuss the iconography of

the whole Gallery but focuses on the place of the planet-gods in the project's original, but, as Stein would claim, never completed plan. Arguing for the project's completion, Kragelund 2006 is the first systematic survey of what is known about the iconography of the entire Gallery.

22   Berg 1646, unpag. begins his list of the Gallery's statues in the bottom, western corner, but is otherwise identical with that of Thurah 1749, 15; Pontoppidan 1764, 307 is once again unwilling to name these heathen divinities "of evil import, but in marble" ("det samme Slags Diviniteter, som jeg tilforn meldte om, slette af Betydning, men i Marmor").

23   Weilbach 1923, III suggests that the statue called JUPITER by Berg and Thurah in fact was a MARS; this is no doubt correct. Steenwinckel/Keyser would have saved Jupiter for the central top position. Mars & Venus is the standard combination, also here.

24   Beckett 1914, 263 lists the statues that survived the fire in 1859 in a reasonable condition; Thorlacius-Ussing 1945, 108 lists their height, but I have been unable to check these measurements.

25   Meldahl's anachronistic emphasis probably gave rise to the suggestion by Christianson 2009, 107 that the Gallery's original imagery focused on the planets (on the top) and the twelve Labours of Hercules (in the two storeys below).

26   Weilbach 1923, III suggests that the statues called ORPHEUS and EURYDICE by Berg and Thurah in fact were Apollo & Diana, but this seems arbitrary. Chiastic male-female arrangement: Kragelund 2006, 54; the reading accepted by Skougaard 2006, 68, Heiberg 2017, 103 and Lyngby 2017, 164–65.

27   Beckett 1914, 132–33 and Skougaard 2006, 65–79 and Cole 2010, 90–94 (the latter with intriguing discussion of contemporary parallels and models) discuss the disposition of the king's and queen's Apartments in the Royal Wing. The visit at Nonsuch is recorded by the diarist quoted ch. III, n. 18; for the original display at Nonsuch, see Biddle 2010, 103–5 and, in particular, Biddle 2012, 336–40; "gilded slate": Biddle 2012, 338.

CHAPTER V

1   De Bray 1631, 23 tab. xlii, "Galderije des Koninghs van Denemercken tot Fredericx-burgh"; the central passage reports: "yder deser vacken of twee boven-een-staende bogen, zijn toe-ge-eygent aen eene der seven Planeet-Goden, 't welcke in yder boge met beeldenisse, en alle soorten van wercken daer op passende wert uyt-gebeeldet, en boven dien komt het beeldt van yder der Planeten selve boven op het opperste van zijn toe-ghewyde boge te staen"; with the generous help of prof. Konrad Ottenheym (*per litteras*), I construe this as meaning: "Each bay of two superimposed arcades is dedicated to one of the seven planet-gods, who in each bay are suitably depicted with reliefs in diverse manners; above these, on top of the upper arcades, is a statue of each of the planet-gods"; Ottenheym informs me that while "bovendien" means "moreover", "boven dien" (in two words) meant "above these" (which of course makes excellent sense). With respect to the caption's twice repeated "beeldenisse" I have modified the translation of Ottenheym 2011, 315–16 slightly, since it now seems clear that De Bray refers to the balustrade's planet-god reliefs.

2   Beckett 1914, 71 reproduces the print and at 263 briefly mentions the planet-god statues and reliefs, but typically shows no interest at all in the iconography; the lack of statues in the niches seems an indication that the drawing is an early Steenwinckel draft that is architecturally precise, whereas its designs for the sculptures are very sketchy: Neurdenburg 1943, 35; Neurdenburg's assumption seems corroborated by the iconographical differences between the drawn and finished

reliefs and statues. In either case, de Keyser and his assistant Gerrit Lambertsen (1597–1657) in the end opted for different solutions. This was customary: Ottenheym 2011, 315.

3 For the relevant iconography, the Iconographic Database of the Warburg Institute gives an excellent survey: http://warburg.sas.ac.uk/vpc/VPC_search/subcats.php?cat_1=9&cat_2=71&cat_3=647&cat_4=992

4 The navy of Christian IV: Bellamy 2006.

5 Neurdenburg 1943, 36 identifies the god as Jupiter, Stein 1972, 287 the goddess as Venus; similarly Bøggild Johannsen & Johannsen 1993, 102 and Kragelund 2006, 58–59.

6 Wade 1996, 177; 332 ill. 116 and Kragelund 2006, 54–61 follow Beckett 1914, 128–29 in concluding that de Keyser delivered the planet-god reliefs as well as the statues; indeed, a visitor to de Keyser's workshop in 1619, an agent of King Christian named Theodorus Rodenburg, reported that he had seen "die besondere beelden en figuuren" (*the remarkable reliefs and statues*) being produced for the Gallery: Ottenheym 2011, 314.

7 Danckerts and de Keyser: Ottenheym 2013, 121. The *Nouveau livre* based upon de Keyser's original drawings for the reliefs: Neurdenburg 1943, 33–41. Their planet-god imagery: Stein 1972, 284–93. Rasbech 1832, 96 reports that six of the Gallery's thirteen reliefs were recut by Axel Øxendal under Christian VI; the prints show that these copies are reasonably faithful to the originals. The present-day, post-Meldahl order of the reliefs is, from west to east, *Mercury*, *Diana*, *Saturn*, *Apollo*, *Venus*, *Jupiter* and *Mars*. *Venus* and *Mars* are the only of the seven in their original position.

8 Fuhring 2004 lists two editions of these prints, the first (nos. 11925–11936) by Cornelis I. Danckerts (1603–56), the second (nos. 11937–11945) by I(ustus) Dan(c)ker(ts) (1635–1701); for a hitherto overlooked third edition, see ch. V, n. 9. Neurdenburg 1943 had access only to a set lacking the original bindings; Stein 1972 drew his knowledge from her publication.

9 I have located six surviving sets of these prints but there may well be more. The first edition published by Neurdenburg in 1943 is now in the Museum Boymans-van Beuningen, Rotterdam: Ottenheym 2011, 323 n. 12. In the Rijksmuseum, there is yet a copy of this first edition, but only nine out of twelve sheets of the second; WorldCat.org further lists a set, be it the first or second edition, that was kept in Halle, but the library kindly informs me that it is lost; finally, there is a set kept in the Herzogin Anna Amaliæ Bibliothek in Weimar, but this is incomplete. It does not have *Saturn*, but according to Fuhring 2004, no. 11939 the original copperplate with *Saturn* in the Rijkmuseum's second edition was clearly damaged and later probably broke – the Weimar plates showing what happened in what turns out to be the, hitherto unknown, *third* edition: *Saturn* was left out and the numbering of the prints was consequently changed, old print 1 becoming new print 1–2 and the rest numbered from 3 to 12 (nos. 3–8 are the remaining six planets, nos. 9–12 more sea-gods), so that it all added up again. To judge from the catalogue, Landesbibliothek Oldenburg has a further complete set of this third edition and so has the Victoria and Albert Museum (with thanks to the museum's curator Sarah Grant for helpful clarification).

10 Hauber 1916 discusses the late medieval manuscripts, Lippmann 1895 the early Renaissance prints that crucially influenced subsequent developments of the iconography.

11 Planets at Palazzo Pitti and at Versailles: Campbell 1977 and Hans 2015.

12 Deppe 2006, 238–312 and Schnitzer 2014, 15–17 survey the very long-lived planet-god symbolism in Dresden court pageants; in 1721, King Augustus of Poland and Saxony named Dresden's seven bastions after the seven planets.

13 Planet-god sculptures: ch. VI, n. 3 (Jonghelinck).

14 Frescoes and reliefs with planet-gods: Fuchs 1909, 35, 44, 58 and Blume 2000, 70 ff. (Giotto's Campanile in Florence, Venice's *Palazzo Ducale*; *Palazzo della Ragione* in Padua and *Palazzo Schifanoia* in Ferrara).

15 Gosslar 2005.
16 Rapp Buri & Stucky-Schürer 2007 and Schmitz-von Ledebur 2009.
17 Among print series, the *Septem planetarum signa et operationes* by Herman Janszen Muller after Maarten van Heemskerck were widely imitated: Veldman 1986, 73–81.
18 Planet-god decorations of burgher houses in Hildesheim, Lübeck, Lüneburg and Nürnberg as well as at the castle in Heidelberg: Behrendsen 1926, von Oechelhaeuser 1923, 162–63 and Stein 1972, 285ff.
19 In planet-god iconography, Apollo's horses are traditional, but his trident (usually Neptune's attribute) is probably a draftsman's error; or perhaps a joke (Apollo at sea?). The driver also holds a trident on the relief.
20 Fuhring 2004, nos. 11925–11945 knows of the link to Frederiksborg, but not of that to the planet-gods; since some of the imagery, for instance the prevalently female drivers, is slightly odd, some of Fuhring's identifications are, understandably, somewhat off the mark.
21 Berg 1646, unpag. "auff den Ründungen sieben andere Bilder, welche, wie alle ob(en) genannte ... nach Lebens grösse in weisse Steine gehauen"; CYBELE etc.: Thurah 1749, 16; similarly, Rasbech 1832, 96.
22 Against Beckett 1914, 128–29 (a lucid summary), Neurdenburg 1943, 37 and Stein 1972, 286–87 argue that the decorative scheme was never completed; neither discusses the evidence for restoration and rearrangements during the eighteenth century: ch. v, n. 7; ch. vii, n. 35–37. Overlooking the evidence of the reliefs and of de Bray (ch. v, n. 1), Lyngby 2017, 163 accepts the list in Thurah 1749, 16 as largely identical with Steenwinckel's original disposition, but fails to discuss the clear discrepancies in style and height between the three surviving de Keyser statues (fig. 5.12, 5.14 and 5.15) and the 30 cm taller Minerva that clearly comes from a different context and workshop: ch. v, n. 24–25.

23 Heräus 1694, 567 reports that the Gallery statues had gilded parts: "dont la face (i.e. of the Royal Wing) est ornée de colonnes et de statues de marbre dorées en quelque endroits."
24 30 cm taller: the admirably thorough Thorlacius-Ussing 1945, 108 lists the height of each statue. Stein 1972, 284–93 and Lyngby 2017, 163 do not take this crucial evidence into account and Neurdenburg 1943 was in the main constrained to work from photographs. For the statues from the bottom tier, the height ranges between 164 and 172 cm; from the middle tier, they are correspondingly lower, between 150 and 154 cm; the difference between de Keyser's *Saturn* (176 cm), *Jupiter* (177 cm) and *Venus* (184 cm) seems acceptable therefore, above all because the proportions and style are so similar; Jupiter would, moreover, originally have been represented with his arm raised, brandishing his thunderbolts.
25 It is a fair assumption that statues such as those from the Tiltyard arch, which was torn down in 1736 (ch. vii, n. 35–37), were reused elsewhere. This may well be the provenance of the so-called "Bacchus", which Thurah a few years later lists as standing among the planet-gods. At the Tiltyard arch, he had an obvious festive function (Berg 1646, unpag.), on the Gallery none. The still preserved *Minerva* may also come from there: ch. vii, n. 37.
26 Thurah 1749, 16 mentions a CYBELE, but also a JUNO; there is no way of determining whether one of these labels refers to the extant statue. Beckett 1914, 127 identified it as a Juno, Weilbach 1923, 112 as Cybele (or Juno) and Neurdenburg 1943, 35 as a Cybele; this latter identification with Cybele/Ops is endorsed by Lyngby 2018, 165–67, but the inference seems arbitrary: the statue has none of the iconographical traits (mural crown/lions) that in the period's art would identify her as Cybele (an iconography perfectly familiar to the artists of Christian iv: fig. 8.6). In discussions of the statue's identity, Stein 1972, 289 is the first to call for an iconographical approach, but his application is somewhat impressionistic and his conclusion

that she is either Juno or Ops does not hold water: ch. v, n. 27–29.
27 Juno or Ops: Stein 1972, 289; Bøggild Johannsen & Johannsen 1993, 102; Stein mentions, but, strangely, does not explain the goats at the goddess' feet; neither does Lyngby 2017, 164; in the period's art, such supports or adornments served as identifiers (cf. *Jupiter*'s eagle and *Cybele*'s mural crown, fig. 5.14; 8.6).
28 Cartari 1581, 452–53; another of the period's famous discussions of iconography (Capaccio 1592, ii, 72) lists a series of ancient parallels for this link between Venus and the goat (*ariete*), among them a renowned statue by Scopas described in Pausanias, *Description of Greece* 6.25.1. The mythological and iconographic tradition (Delivorrias 1984, 98–100) sometimes describes the animal as a goat, but elsewhere as a heifer; what matters is the repeated emphasis on a link between Venus and animals with these characteristic curved horns: Kragelund 2006, 58–59; Lyngby 2017, 164 returns to Stein's identification (ch. v, n. 26–27) with Ops without, however, addressing, let alone quoting, the iconographical evidence presented in Kragelund 2006, 58–59, which shows the identification to be untenable.
29 Thus Wade 1996, 177; 332 ill.116 and Kragelund 2006, 54–61 followed by Ottenheym, Rosenberg & Smit 2008, 118–19, Ottenheym 2011, 313 and Heiberg 2017, 106. Lyngby 2017, 163–65 and 2018, 160–67 rejects the proposed planet-god programme and takes the group listed in Thurah 1749, 16 as largely identical with the group put up by Steenwinckel. In view of the abundant and unanimous near-contemporary evidence to the contrary, the argument will not stand.
30 Mellbye-Hansen 1986 documents the continued intervention of restorers between the period of Thurah and the fire in 1859. Meldahl's post-fire drawing in the Danish National Art Library (inv. no. 53385q) has the statues in the same order as on Lund's painting in the Frederiksborg Museum (inv. no. A 9368); this painting and its sketches (inv. nos. A 5009; 5010 (both dated June 1858) and 6020 (dated 1861)) show *Jupiter* precisely where the post-fire photo has him (fig. 5.18). The photo is blurred, but the stump of *Jupiter*'s right arm, the curve of his body and his eagle's left wing make identification certain.

CHAPTER VI

1 The position of the Mars relief: Beckett 1914, 263.
2 Heräus 1694, 567 (ch. v, n. 23) reports that the Gallery statues were partly gilded (presumably crowns, jewellery and other attributes).
3 Jonghelinck's planet-gods: Meijer 1979, 116–35 and Buchanan 1990, 102–13.
4 On the king's politics, Heiberg 2017 (with ample bibliography) is the modern standard account.
5 Friis 1872–78, 273; Stein 1972, 286.

CHAPTER VII

1 Stags' heads: Bligaard 1984, 66; "lead nowhere": Cole 2010, 90 n. 133; Somerset House: Thurley 2009, 43; chronology stands in the way of assuming (as Skovgaard 1973, 129 already had done) that King Christian brought back the idea for the Privy Gallery from his second visit in 1614. By 1612 the Privy Gallery and the Audience House were already under way: Beckett 1914, 168–69. But exchange between the royal brother and sister was lively (five musicians for instance sent from Denmark to

Anne's court orchestra: Meikle & Payne 2004, 198), so there may well have been letters now lost; none of the letters from Anne to her brother and others in Denmark in Rigsarkivet seem relevant here (with thanks to Jørgen Hein for references).

2   Richmond and its gardens: Thurley 1993, plan 11; Coope 1986 surveys the origins and function of the English "Long Gallery"; Christian IV at Richmond 7 August 1606: Roberts 1606b = Nichols 1828, vol. II, 81. For such connecting galleries at Hampton Court, see Thurley 2013, 215–16.

3   Christian IV at Whitehall 1–2 August 1606: Roberts 1606b = Nichols 1828, vol. II, 79; he arrived by barge from the Tower and on 2 August hunted in St. James' Park, so he would have seen Whitehall from the river as well as from the park; the function of the Holbein Gate: Thurley 1999, 45–47; Thurley 2017, 134–35.

4   At a conference in January 2017 in the Society of Antiquaries in London, Emily Cole generously informed me of these new findings and allowed me to consult and quote her then unpublished study: Cole 2017, 92–93; the impact on Frederiksborg: Cole 2017, 107–8.

5   Münzberg 2007.

6   Geometry: Wanscher 1937, 90–91; Randsborg 2004, 15 (both with fine measurings). Their attempt to resurrect the old story of Inigo Jones' involvement is implausible, and the use of geometry proves nothing: the technique was rooted in medieval tradition: Schepelern 1973, 42; Velte 1951; Naredi-Rainer 1982 (an objection neither met by Wanscher nor Randsborg). Bligaard 1984, 56–57 rightly observes that the joining together of the Gallery and Audience House is remarkably inept; similarly, Neumann 2011, 67–68.

7   For the double apartment, see Paulson 1958, 114–16; Cole 2010, 89 ff. and Albrecht 2011, 202–17 (the latter with intriguing manor-house parallels); for Güstrow, which Christian visited in 1595, see Erbentraut 1999, 27–40; on the French court ceremonial, see Boudon & Chatenet 1994, 65–82; as rightly outlined by Cole 2010, 88, the Danish ceremonial seems more akin to the Bavarian (in its origin Burgundian: Baillie 1967, 198–99) ceremonial studied by Klingensmith 1993, 12–13; 27–36; for the increasing importance of the ceremonial aspect of court life of the period, see further Thurley 2012 (with bibliography) and ch. VIII, n. 1.

8   Alstrup 2013.

9   Greenwich: Dyson 1606, 8 with Thurley 2017, 99–101; Dresden: ch. VII, n. 14 and 21 and fig. 7.21 and 7.23; on the Tiltyard at Frederiksborg recent studies add nothing to the very basic summary by Beckett 1914, 167–72. At the Royal Palace in Copenhagen, Resen's bird's-eye view from 1674 shows a Tiltyard with adjoining "Judicir- und Wagenhäusser" just to the west of the old palace, but the date and layout of this lost complex is badly documented: Friis 1947, 23.

10 Resen's *Atlas* is based upon a complex compilation process: Hertig 1994, 9–18.

11 "Additur hic curriculum Trojanis, quos vocant, lusibus destinatum; est ibi videre splendidam, ut ap(p)ellant, aedem judicii, extructos affabre arcus, inauratos obeliscos, frequentes colossiaeos, Deorum Dearumq. simulacra, felici adeo veterum aemulatione efficta, ut arte hodiernorum victa antiquitas suis pene inventis erubescat", *Petri Resenii Atlas Danicus*, tom. ii, 379, Ulldall 186 fol., The Royal Danish Library.

12 I am indebted to the late Hugo Johannsen for the suggestion, years back, to look closer into the architecture of tiltyards in order to understand the layout at Frederiksborg.

13 In 1623 a princely guest (Krause 1858, 101) was shown the 120 silver cups King Christian had won in runnings at the ring: Friis 1877, 27; Hein 2006, 53.

14 EQVORVM: thus the inscription above the arch leading from the north into the Dresden *Turnierhof*; the Dresden ceremonial and site: Watanabe-O'Kelly 2002, 43–70; Syndram 2012, 139–42.

15 In modern Berlin, the street name *An der Stechbahn* still reflects the original function of the area to the south of the palace.

NOTES   179

16 On *Ringrennen* at Protestant courts, Watanabe-O'Kelly 1992, 37–63 and Wade 2003 are excellent surveys; Holst 1635, unpag. has a set of nineteen rules for such a game (a section not included in the transcript in Mulryne 2004, vol. II, 273–91); the Berlin print (fig. 7.8) is discussed in detail in Peschken & Klünner 1982, 34–35. Bruun 1872–73 publishes an anonymous report from 1663 which i.a. describes three days of such competitions during the celebrations of a royal wedding in Copenhagen. Friis 1947 surveys developments in Denmark until c.1790, when such competitions finally went out of fashion.

17 The Copenhagen print is discussed in detail by Wade 1996, 45 ff.

18 King Christian stayed in contact with Nosseni: in 1615 he ordered four marble fireplaces for Frederiksborg: Mackowsky 1904, 100–1.

19 Roberts 1606b, unpag. = Nichols 1828, vol. II, 80.

20 For the centrality of this concept in the period's view of the monarch, see: Hein 2006a, 213–30, Hein 2009, 32 and Heiberg 2017, 217.

21 Dresden judge box: Syndram 2012, 24; 140; Berlin: fig. 7.8.

22 Berg 1646, unpag. "ein herrlich Judicirhaus zusehn, so von rothen gebran(n)ten Steinen aufgemauret"; Resen 1688, 379, "splendidam … aedem judicii"; still described as the original "Judiceerhus" by Rasbech 1832, 80.

23 Resen would not have praised the *Judicirhaus* as "splendidam", if it had simply been red-brick; to Berg 1646, unpag. the Audience House is likewise a "herrliches Haus" (with no specific reference to its sculptures). Jessen c.1765 (unpaginated, but at the end of the mss) confirms that the *Judicirhaus* "roughly thirty years back still" (*endnu for henimod 30 Aar siden*) had been adorned with statues.

24 Rasbech 1832, 80 and the map in Becker & Richardt 1852 confirm that the former so-called "Judiceerhus" was still standing. Meldahl admits to having pulled it down: Meldahl 1887, 62; an act strongly criticised by Beckett 1914, 167; 239, Weilbach 1923, 88 and Weilbach 1929, 74–76. The antiquarian J. J. A. Worsaa had demanded that the building was carefully documented before being torn down, but sadly these drawings seem lost: Eller 1964, 133–34. Modern discussions tend to reproduce plans of the castle "in the days of Christian IV", as if the *Judicirhaus* had never existed (thus e.g. the museum's video (cf. ch. IV, n. 3) illustrating the building history of Frederiksborg).

25 Steenberg 1950, 46; 156–57 misreads Jessen c.1765 when claiming that the whole *Judicirhaus* had been pulled down in c.1685: cf. ch. VII, n. 23.

26 In an engraving after Roed, Weilbach 1929, 74–76 saw traces of three walled-up arcades, but neither in the engraving nor the original painting can I see any such traces. And the photo (fig. 7.17) proves that there were none. Holm's watercolour is at Frederiksborg: A 1276.

27 The pre-fire watercolour is probably a sketch for a painting listed in *Catalog…1902* no. 11, "Frederiksborg Slot set fra Ridebanen. Malet før Branden. 1858." For the accuracy of Lund's drawings of the Marble Gallery, see ch. V, n. 30 and fig. 5.18.

28 Cf. Geyer 1936, fig. 24; fig. 105; in a painting by Hans Knieper of the original Frederiksborg from 1580–84, one sees a similar horse pool on the south-eastern side of the castle's first island: Ragn Jensen 2006, 85.

29 Queen Anne in the window: Anon., *The Mar(r)iage* 1613, 7; cf. Nichols 1828, vol. II, 549.

30 Young 1987, 206–7.

31 Layout of the tiltyards at Greenwich, Richmond, Hampton Court and Whitehall: Young 1987, 101–22; Thurley 1993, plan 2 (Greenwich); Thurley 2017, 99–100 (tiltyard towers at Greenwich).

32 Stone balustrade: Nicolai 1769, 57.

33 Skovgaard's painting: Larsen 2013, 45; the facade was slightly changed in the 1830s, but for painterly effect Skovgaard may well have chosen to ignore this; traces on the stable walls strongly suggest that there was such loggia decoration: Beckett 1918, plate 32.

34 "inauratos obeliscos", Resen (ch. VII, n. 11).

35 In 1736 Steenwinckel's richly adorned tiltyard arch was torn down and replaced by the present, much simpler structure: Beckett 1914, 206–7; Weilbach 1923, 38, 57; unlike Beckett, the architect Vilhelm Holck saw no reason to doubt that the dimensions and form of the present arch are very like the original: Beckett 1918 on pl. 36–37.

36 Thurahs description of the "so-called tiltyard" pointedly abstains from mentioning the restored arch: Thurah 1749, 56–57. His criticism: Beckett 1914, 207.

37 The surviving *Minerva* that ended up on the top of the Gallery may have come from this arch: it is 204 cm tall.

38 Berg 1646, unpag., "eine grosse Pforte von weissen Quarterstein, auff derer Seiten zween Schwiebogen erbauet. Zur Rechten an der Pforten stehen Ceres und Bacchus, zur Lincken Sol und Luna, niederwerts auff der andern Seiten Pallas und Mars, zur Lincken Venus und Hercules. Oben auff der Pforten Ründung Neptunus nebenst dem zur Rechten Jupiter und Juno, zur Lincken Pluto und Proserpina; sind zusammen nach Lebens grösse in weisse Quarterstein gehauen, auff steinern Postementen gesetzet, an vielen Orten mit halbgeschlagenem Golde überzogen. Auff der Schwiebogen Ründungen, beydes zur Rechten und Lincken, halten vier Bilder das Königliche wap(p)en, ebenmässig in weissen Steinen gehauen und vergüldet."

39 Larsson 1967, 73 notes *Neptune*'s eminence, but sees no thematic reason for it; Lyngby & Skougaard 2009, 50 suggest a parallel to the Fountain; similarly Lyngby 2017, 170 (but what would be the point?); the *ludi Troiani* and the obelisks (and their associations) go unmentioned.

40 *Lusus Troiae*: Erskine 2001, 19–20.

41 Consus/Neptune and *Circus Maximus*: Livy, *History of Rome* 1.9.7; Plutarch, *Life of Romulus* 14.3–5; Servius' commentary on Vergil's *Aeneid* 8.635–36.

42 Obelisks standing in ancient Rome's circuses: Pliny, *Naturalis Historia* 16.201; 36.71; Ammianus Marcellinus, *History of Rome* 17.4 (the Vatican and *Circus Maximus*) with Iversen 1968, 21–23 and 55–75; in the Renaissance, drawings and prints also circulated of the obelisk at the Circus of Maxentius later to be re-erected in Piazza Navona: Iversen 1968, 82–83.

43 Panvinio 1600, pl. 32 and 50 reproduces Roman imperial medals illustrating the ancient use of triumphal arches as the entry to a circus; the brothers Steenwinckel's copy of Dietterlin at the Royal Danish Library: Beckett 1914, 171. Its arch has Minerva, the nine Muses and Pegasus. In Steenwinckel's version on the Audience House, the inserted cartouche with Mars and Venus meant that the Pegasus and four of the nine Muses had to be left out.

44 Ovid, *Metamorphoses* 5.336, "nemorisque levi consedit in umbra." Bramsen 1982, 63 mistakenly claims that the motif is Biblical; for the illustrated Ovid editions (also with Minerva to the left, the Muses to the right), see the entries in Huber-Rebenich et al. 2014, B 177–78 and in the Warburg Iconographic database, https://iconographic.warburg.sas.ac.uk/vpc/VPC_search/subcats.php?cat_1=5&cat_2=115&cat_3=98&cat_4=60. Beckett 1914, 171 and Stein 1987, 90 rightly identify the motif, but have nothing on the links to Ovid and his *Nachleben*. Lyngby 2017, 172 describes the group as Minerva and musicians, he too with no reference to Ovid.

45 The group (here identified as an *Actaeon*) is described by Thurah 1749, 60; Lund 2000, 154 convincingly dates the fountain to about 1720.

46 Wade 2003a (with bibliography) is excellent in tracing the way the sibling links between these Protestant courts facilitated cultural exchange.

47 Anne played the lute and entertained visitors with her own orchestra: Meikle & Payne 2004, 198; the French lute player Charles de Lespine compared the generosity of King Christian with that of his late sister: Lachèvre 1935, 120; her fountain: Strong 1979, 87–92; Morgan 2007, 115–21.

48 Nichols 1828, vol. III, 16 (31 July 1614).

49 Decorating the Audience House started in June 1614: Beckett 1914, 172–73.

50 Stein 1987, 90–108.

ENVOI

1. Music at the Danish Court: Spohr 2012; for ceremonial at European courts, see ch. VII, n. 7; developing the typology established by Bauer 1993, Olden Jørgensen 2002 surveys developments under Frederik II and Christian IV; Bøggild Johannsen & Ottenheym 2015 survey related changes in the period's court settings (with extensive bibliography).

2. Ceremonial at Theobalds and in London: Sutton 2004; Shapiro 2015, 289–317; at Dresden: Watanabe-O'Kelly 2002; Deppe 2006; in general: Wade 2003–2003a.

3. Eller 1975 surveys the evidence for the anointments that started with Christian V and ended with Christian VIII in 1841; of the seven absolutist kings, only the mentally ill Christian VII remained in Copenhagen for his anointment.

Bibliography

MANUSCRIPTS

Rigsarkivet (The National Archives, Copenhagen)

Tyske Kancelli, *Udenrigske Anliggender, England*, AI, nr. 2, Breve 1602–25, Letters from Anne.

Tyske Kancelli, *Udenrigske Anliggender, Skotland*, AI, nr. 2, Breve 1567–1603, Letters from Anne.

The Royal Danish Library, Department of Manuscripts

Anon., *Kongelig Maiettz Reigsse till Engellanndt Anno 1606*, diary (in Danish) of a courtier accompanying Christian IV on his visit to England in 1606, *Ny Kgl. Samling* 364c, 2° (transcript kindly provided by Dr Cay Dollerup).

Gerner, Henrik Thomsen, (1629–1700), *Det viidt berømte Friderichsborgs Beskrivelse*, mss from c.1680, *Thott* 1390, 4°, pp. 167–230.

Jessen, E.J., *Frederiksborg Amts Naturlige= og Civile Tilstand* (c.1765), *Kall*, 48, II, fol.

Resen, Peder Hansen, *Atlas Danicus sive Descriptio Regni Daniae*, mss from 1688, *Ulldall* 186 2°.

BOOKS AND ARTICLES

Airs, Malcolm, "'Pomp or Glory': The Influence of Theobalds," in: Pauline Croft (ed.), *Patronage, Culture and Power: The Early Cecils*, Yale 2002, 3–19.

Albrecht, Uwe, "Renaissance-Architektur des westlichen Ostseeraumes im Spiegel von Traktat und Musterbuch: Kalmar, Kronborg, Frederiksborg," in: Krista Kodres (ed.), *The Problem of the Classical Ideal in the Art and Architecture of the Countries around the Baltic Sea*, Tallinn 2003, 13–31.

Albrecht, Uwe, "Deutsche, französische und niederländische Einflüsse als Wegbereiter und Katalysatoren der dänischen Renaissance-Architektur in der zweiten Hälfte des 16. Jahrhunderts", in: Andersen, Bøggild Johannsen & Johannsen 2011, 197–218.

Alstrup, Kent, "*Et in Arcadia ego.*" Barokinteriørerne i Audienshuset på Frederiksborg Slot, online publication, Slotte & Kulturejendomme, 2013.

Andersen, Michael, Ebbe Nyborg & Mogens Vedsø (eds.), "Renaissance Art and Architecture in Denmark," in: Michael Andersen, Ebbe Nyborg & Mogens Vedsø (eds.), *Masters, Meanings & Models*, Copenhagen 2010, 23–31.

Andersen, Michael, Birgitte Bøggild Johannsen & Hugo Johannsen (eds.), *Reframing the Danish Renaissance: Problems and Prospects in a European Perspective*, Copenhagen 2011.

Andrews, Martin, "Theobalds Palace: The Gardens and Park," *Garden History* 21 (1993) 129–49.

Anon., *Catalog over Malerier ... af ... F.C. Lund, 10/2 1902*, Copenhagen 1902.

Anon., *The Mar(r)iage of Prince Fredericke, and the Kings daughter, the Lady Elizabeth upon Shrouesunday last*, London 1613.

Baagøe, Jette, *Kongens Skov. Verdens Arv. Parforcejagtlandskabet I Nordsjælland/ The King's Forest. The World's Heritage. The Par Force Hunting Landscape in North Zealand*, Dansk Jagt- og Skovbrugsmuseum 2015.

Baillie, Hugh Murray, "Etiquette and the Planning of the State Apartments in Baroque Palaces," *Archaeologia* 101 (1967) 169–99.

Bartetzky, Arnold, "Hans Vredeman de Vries' geschweifte Beschlagwerkgiebeln. Zu ihrer Herkunft, Aneignung und Verbreitung in der Architektur Mittel- und Nordeuropas", in: Borggrefe & Lüpkes 2005, 75–82.

Bauer, Volker, *Die höfische Gesellschaft in Deutschland von der Mitte des 17. bis zum Ausgang des 18. Jahrhunderts. Versuch einer Typologie*, Tübingen 1993.

Beard, Mary, *Twelve Caesars: Images of Power from Ancient Rome to Salvador Dalí*, The Sixtieth A.W. Mellon Lectures in the Fine Arts. Online at www.nga.gov from 2014.

Becker, T. A. & F. Richardt, *Prospekter af Kongelige Slotte, gamle og nye, … I, Frederiksborg Slot,* Copenhagen 1852.

Beckett, Francis, *Frederiksborg I, Opmaalinger*, Copenhagen 1918.

Beckett, Francis, *Frederiksborg II, Slottets Historie*, Copenhagen 1914.

Bedoire, Frederic, *Guldålder. Slott och Politik i 1600-talets Sverige*, Stockholm 2001.

Behrendsen, Otto, *Darstellungen von Planetengottheiten an und in deutschen Bauten*, Strassburg 1926.

Bellamy, Martin J., *Christian IV and His Navy: A Political and Administrative History of the Danish Navy, 1596–1648*, Boston 2006.

Berg, Johan Adam, *Kurtze und eigentliche Beschreibung des fürtrefflichen und weitberühmten Königlichen Hauses Friederichsburg*, Copenhagen 1646.

Biddle, Martin, "The Gardens at Nonsuch: Sources and Dating," *Garden History* 27 (1999) 145–83.

Biddle, Martin, "'Makinge of moldes for the walles': The Stuccoes of Nonsuch: Materials, Methods and Origins", in: Rune Frederiksen & Eckart Marchand (eds.), *Plaster Casts: Making, Collecting and Displaying from Classical Antiquity to the Present*, Berlin 2010, 99–117.

Biddle, Martin, "Nonsuch, Henry VIII's Mirror for a Prince: Sources and Interpretation," in: Cinzia Maria Sicca & Louis A. Waldman (eds.), *The Anglo-Florentine Renaissancee: Art for the Early Tudors*, New Haven 2012, 307–50.

Bligaard, Mette, "The Privy Passage and the Audience House at Frederiksborg Palace," *Leids Kunsthistorisch Jaerboek* 1984, 55–68.

Bligaard, Mette, *Frederiksborgs genrejsning. Historicisme i teori og praksis*, vol. I–II, Copenhagen 2008.

Blondel, François, *La Solitude Royalle, ou Description de Friderisbourg*, Copenhagen 1653.

Blume, Dieter, *Regenten des Himmels. Astrologische Bilder in Mittelalter und Renaissance*, Berlin 2000.

Blunt, Anthony, *Art and Architecture in France 1500–1700*, New Haven 1999.

Borggrefe, Heiner & Vera Lüpkes (eds.), *Hans Vredeman de Vries und die Folgen*, Marburg 2005.

Boudon, Françoise & Monique Chatenet, "Les logis du roi de France au XVIe siècle," in: Jean Guillaume (ed.), *Architecture et vie sociale: l'organisation intérieure des grandes demeures à la fin du Moyen Age et à la Renaissance,* actes du colloque tenu à Tours du 6 au 10 juin 1988, Paris 1994, 65–82.

Bramsen, Henrik, *Symbolik i Christian den Fjerdes arkitektur*, Copenhagen 1982.

Bray, Salomon de, *Architectura Moderna*, Amsterdam 1631.

Bruun, Chr., "Kurfyrstinde Magdalene Sibylla og Kurprinds Johan Georg af Sachsens Rejse til Danmark 1663," *Danske Samlinger for Historie, Topografi, Personal- og Litteraturhistorie* 2. Rk., 2 (1872–73) 144–77.

Buchanan, Iain, "The Collection of Niclaes Jongelinck: I. 'Bacchus and the Planets' by Jacques Jongelinck," *The Burlington Magazine* 132 (1990) 102–13.

Buri, Anna Rapp & Monica Stucky-Schürer, *Die Sieben Planeten und ihre Kinder. Eine 1547–1549 datierte Tapisseriefolge*, Basel 2007.

Campbell, Malcom, *Pietro Cortona at the Pitti Palace: A Study of the Planetary Rooms and Related Projects*, Princeton 1977.

Capaccio, Giulio Cesare, *Delle imprese trattato*, Napoli 1592.

Cartari, Vincenzo, *Le imagini de i dei degli antichi*, Lyon 1581.

Cecil Calendar = *Calendar of the Cecil Papers in Hatfield House*, vol. 18, 1606, London 1940 (accessible via British History Online).

Christensen, Charlotte, "Adriaen de Vries' Neptunspringvand", in: Heiberg 2006, 155–172.

Christianson, John Robert, "Terrestrial and Celestial Spaces of the Danish Court, 1550–1650," in: Marcello Fantoni et al. (eds.), *The Politics of Space: European Courts ca. 1500–1750*, Rome 2009, 91–118.

Cole, Emily, *The State Apartment in the Jacobean Country House 1603–1625*, DPhil thesis, September 2010, available at http://sro.sussex.ac.uk/.

Cole, Emily, "Theobalds, Hertfordshire: The Plan and Interiors of an Elizabethan Country House," *Architectural History* 60 (2017) 71–116.

Coope, Rosalys, "'The Long Gallery': Its Origins, Development, Use and Decoration," *Architectural History* 29 (1986) 43–84.

Degn, Ole, *Christian 4.s kansler, Christen Friis til Kragerup (1581–1639)*, Viborg 1988.

Delivorrias, Angelos, "Aphrodite," *Lexicon iconographicum mythologiae classicae*, vol. II, Munich 1984, 2–151.

Deppe, Uta, *Die Festkultur am Dresdner Hofe Johann Georgs II. von Sachsen (1660–1679)*, Kiel 2006.

Dewes, Eva, *Freierprobe und Liebesäpfel. Der Mythos von Atalante und Hippomenes in der Kunst und seine interdisziplinäre Rezeption*, Petersberg 2011.

Dombrowski, Damian, "La regina di Saba al Castello di Dresden," in: Ebert-Schifferer 2007, 37–56.

Dunlop, Ian, *Palaces & Progresses of Elizabeth I*, London 1962.

[Dyson, Humphrey], *The King of Denmarkes welcome: containing his arrivall, abode, and entertainement*, London 1606.

Ebert-Schifferer, Sybille (ed.), *Scambio culturale con il nemico religioso: Italia e Sassonia attorno al 1600*, Cinisello Balsamo 2007.

Eller, Povl, "Frederiksborgs restaurering," in: H.D. Schepelern, Jørgen Paulsen & Poul Eller (eds.), *Omkring Frederiksborg Slots brand*, Hillerød 1964, 107–54.

Eller, Povl, *Salvingerne på Frederiksborg*, Hillerød 1976.

Erbentraut, Regina, *Schloss Güstrow*, Schwerin 1999.

Erskine, Andrew, *Troy between Greece and Rome: Local Tradition and Imperial Power*, Oxford 2001.

Fittschen, Klaus, "Die zwölf suetonischen Kaiser in den Büstengalerien der Renaissance und des Barock," in: Dietrich Boschung & Christiane Vorster (eds.), *Leibhafte Kunst. Statuen und kulturelle Identität*, Paderborn 2015, 201–22.

Ford, John, *The Monarchs meeting, or the King of Denmarkes welcome*, London 1606.

Friis, Frederik Reinholdt, *Samlinger til Dansk Bygnings- og Kunsthistorie*, Copenhagen 1872–78.

Friis, Frederik Reinholdt, *Frederiksborg Slot i det 17de Aarhundrede*, Copenhagen 1877.

Friis, Hjalmar, *Den Kongelige Stald-Etat*, Copenhagen 1947.

Fuchs, Bruno Archibald, *Die Ikonographie der 7 Planeten in der Kunst Italiens bis zum Ausgang des Mittelalters*, Munich 1909.

Fuhring, Peter, *Ornament Prints in the Rijksmuseum II, The Seventeenth Century*, vol. 3, Rotterdam 2004.

Geyer, Albert, *Geschichte des Schlosses zu Berlin*, vol. I–II, Berlin 1936.

Gosslar, Anna, *Paolo Fiammingos Bilderzyklus der sieben Planeten*, Grin Verlag 2005.

Guillaume, Jean, Peter Fuhring & Valérie Auclair et al. (eds.), *Jacques Androuet du Cerceau – "un des plus grands architectes qui se soient jamais trouvés en France,"* Paris 2010.

Hans, Pierre-Xavier (ed.), *Le Salon de Mercure, Chambre de Parade du Roi*, Versailles 2015.

Hauber, Anton, *Planetenkinderbilder und Sternbilder*, Strassburg 1916.

Heaton, Gabriel, *Writing and Reading Royal Entertainments*, Oxford 2010.

Heiberg, Steffen, *Christian 4. En europæisk statsmand*, Copenhagen 2017.

Heiberg, Steffen, "Art and the Staging of Images of Power: Christian IV and Pictorial Art," in: Noldus & Roding 2007, 231–44.

Heiberg, Steffen (ed.), *Christian 4 og Frederiksborg*, Copenhagen 2006.

Hein 2006 = Jørgen Hein, "Christian 4. og reputationen," in: Jørgen Hein, Katia Johansen & Peter Kristiansen (eds.), *Christian 4. og Rosenborg 1606–2006*, Copenhagen 2006, 51–68.

Hein 2006a = Jørgen Hein, "Paradesamlingen på Sparepenge," in: Heiberg 2006, 213–30.

Hein, Jørgen, *The Treasure Collection at Rosenborg Castle*, vol. I–III, Copenhagen 2009.

Henderson, Paula, "The Loggia in Tudor and Early Stuart England: The Adaption and Function of Classical Form," in: Lucy Gent (ed.), *Albion's Classicism: The Visual Arts in Britain, 1550–1660*, Yale 1995, 109–45.

Henderson, Paula, *The Tudor House and Garden: Architecture and Landscape in the Sixteenth and Early Seventeenth Centuries*, New Haven & London 2005.

Henderson, Paula, reviewing Sutton 2004, *Journal of British Studies* 45 (2006) 401–3.

Heräus 1694 = Joseph Bergmann (ed.), "Aus dem Micellenband mit dem Titel "Correspondentia" I, Fragment von Heräus' Reise von Hamburg nach Schweden, im Frühlinge 1694," in: *Sitzb. d. phil.-hist. Classe d. Kais. Akad. d. Wissenschaften* 13 (1854) 564–71.

Hertig, Henrik (ed.), *Resens Atlas: Sjælland*, Odense 1994.

Holst, Jørgen Jørgensen, *Triumphus Nuptialis Danicus*, Copenhagen 1635, unpag.

Howes, Edmund, *The Annales, or generall Chronicle of England, begun first by maister John Stow, and after him continued … by Edmund Howes, gentleman*, London 1615.

Huber-Rebenich, Gerlinde, Sabine Lütkemeyer & Hermann Walter, *Ikonographisches Repertorium zu den Metamorphosen des Ovid. Die textbegleitende Druckgraphik* I.1–I.2, Berlin 2014.

Husselby, Jill & Paula Henderson, "Location, Location, Location! Cecil House in the Strand," *Architectural History* 45 (2002) 159–93.

Ilsøe, Harald, *Udlændinges Rejser i Danmark indtil år 1700*, Copenhagen 1963.

Ilsøe, Harald, "En rejse gennem Danmark på Chr. IV's tid," *Fra Frederiksborg Amt* 1965, 7–17.

Ilsøe, Harald, "Udlændinges Rejser i Danmark indtil år 1700 … Bidrag til en ajourføring," *Fund og Forskning* 54 (2015) 235–51.

Iversen, Erik, *Obelisks in Exile,* vol. I, Copenhagen 1968.

Jensen, Hannemarie Ragn, "Christian 4.s malerier," in: Heiberg 2006, 81–97.

Johannsen, Birgitte Bøggild & Hugo Johannsen, "Kongens kunst," in: Peter Michael Hornung (ed.), *Ny dansk Kunsthistorie*, vol. II, Copenhagen 1993.

Johannsen, Birgitte Bøggild & Konrad Ottenheym (eds.), *Beyond Scylla and Charybdis: European Courts and Court Residences outside Habsburg and Valois/Bourbon Territories 1500–1700*, Copenhagen 2015.

Johannsen, Hugo, "Frederiksborg Slotskirke," in: Erik Moltke et al. (eds.), *Danmarks Kirker* II, *Frederiksborg Amt*, vol. III, Copenhagen 1970, 1673–1926.

Johannsen, Hugo, "Regna Firmat Pietas. Eine Deutung der Baudekoration der Schlosskirche Christians IV zu Frederiksborg," *Hafnia* 1974, 67–140.

Johannsen, Hugo, "On the Significance of Hans Vredeman de Vries for Architecture, Arts and Crafts during the reigns of Frederick II and Christian IV," in: Borggrefe & Lüpkes 2005, 42–49.

Johannsen, Hugo, "The Saxon Connection: On the Architectural Genesis of Christian IV's Palace Chapel (1606–1617) at Frederiksborg Castle," in: Andersen, Nyborg & Vedsø 2010, 71–88.

Johannsen, Hugo, "The Steenwinckels: The Success Story of a Netherlandish Immigrant Family in Denmark," in: Ottenheym & Jonge 2013, 129–42.

Kappel, Jutta & Claudia Brink, *Mit Fortuna übers Meer. Sachsen und Dänemark – Ehen und Allianzen im Spiegel der Kunst (1548–1709)*, Munich 2009.

Keller, Katrin, *Kurfürstin Anna von Sachsen 1532–1585*, Regensburg 2010.

Klingensmith, Samuel John, *The Utility of Splendor: Ceremony, Social Life, and Architecture at the Court of Bavaria, 1600–1800*, Chicago & London 1993.

Kommer, Bjørn R., *Adriaen de Vries. Augsburgs Glanz – Europas Ruhm*, Heidelberg 2000.

Kragelund, Patrick, "Olympens guder," in: Heiberg 2006, 43–61.

Kragelund, Patrick, "Tradition, Ceremony and Innovation: Royal Travels and the Building of Frederiksborg and Rosenborg," in: Steffen Heiberg, Juliette Roding, Poul Holstein & Rolof Höwel tot Westerflier (eds.), *Christian IV and the Crisis of the Danish Monarchy*, Amsterdam 2019.

Krause, Georg (ed.), *Tagebuch Christians des Jüngeren, Fürst zu Anhalt*, Leipzig 1858.

Lachèvre, Frédéric (ed.), *Un joueur de luth et compositeur des cours principières, auteur dramatique et poète Charles de Lespine*, Paris 1935.

Larsen, Lene G., *Frederiksborg Slot. Bygningshistorisk undersøgelse, august 2012–februar 2013*; report commissioned by the SLKE.

Larsson, Lars Olof, *Adrian de Vries 1545–1626*, Vienna & Munich 1967.

Lee, Jr., Maurice (ed.), *Dudley Carleton to John Chamberlain 1603–1624. Jacobean Letters*, New Jersey 1972.

Lippmann, Friedrich, *The Seven Planets*, London 1895.

Lorenzen, Vilhelm, "Arkitekturen," in: Knud Fabricius et al. (eds.), *Holland Danmark*, Copenhagen 1945, 397–487.

Lund, Hakon, *Danmarks Havekunst* 1, Copenhagen 2000.

Lyngby, Thomas & Mette Skougaard, *Frederiksborg Castle and Museum*, Hillerød 2009.

Lyngby, Thomas, "Antikkens guder og helte på Frederiksborg," in: Camilla Plesner Horster & Lærke Maria Andersen Funder (eds.), *Antikkens veje til renæssancens Danmark*, Aarhus 2017, 153–79.

Lyngby, Thomas, "Marmorgalleriet på Frederiksborg Slot," *Carlsbergfondets Årsskrift 2018*, 160–67.

Mackowsky, Walter, *Giovanni Maria Nosseni und die Renaissance in Sachsen*, Berlin 1904.

Meijer, Bert, "The Re-emergence of a Sculptor: Eight Lifesize Bronzes by Jacques Jonghelinck," *Oud Holland* 93 (1979) 116–35.

Meikle, Maureen M. & Helen Payne, "Anne," *Oxford Dictionary of National Biography,* vol. 11, 2004, 191–99.

Meldahl, Ferdinand, *Beretning om Frederiksborg Slots Gjenopførelse og Restaurering efter Branden d. 17. December 1859*, Copenhagen 1887.

Mellbye-Hansen, Preben, *Hovedporten og terrassemuren på Frederiksborg Slot*, unpublished report, Boligministeriet 1988, unpag.

Montecuccoli 1654 = Raimondo Montecuccoli, *I viaggi. Opera inedita pubblicata a cura di Adriano Gimorri*, Modena 1924.

Morgan, Luke, *Nature as Model: Salomon de Caus and Early Seventeenth-Century Landscape Design*, Philadelphia 2007.

Mulryne, James R., et al. (eds.), *Europa Triumphans*, vol. II, London 2004.

Münzberg, Esther, "*Aula enim principis non equorum videbatur* – Der neue Stall- und Harnischkammerbau in Dresden 1586," in: Ebert-Schifferer 2007, 143–51.

v. Naredi-Rainer, Paul, *Architektur und Harmonie. Zahl, Mass und Proportion in der abendländischen Baukunst*, Cologne 1982.

Neumann, Jens Martin, "... 'gewinnt der Stil seine Eigenart': Schloss Frederiksborg. Überlegungen zur Autonomie und Originalität nordischer Renaissance," *Nordelbingen* 80 (2011) 57–80.

Neurdenburg, Elisabeth, "Hendrick de Keyser en het beeldhouwwerk aan de galerij van Frederiksborg in Denemarken," *Oudheidkundig Jaarboek* 1943, 33–41.

Neville, Davis H., "The Limitations of Festival: Christian IV's State Visit to England in 1606," in: J. R. Mulryne & Margaret Shewring (eds.), *Italian*

Renaissance Festivals and their European Influence, Lewiston, New York 1992, 311–35.

Nichols, John, *The Progresses, Processions, and Magnificent Festivities, of King James the First,* vol. I–IV, London 1828.

Nicolai, Friedrich, *Bescreibung der Königlichen Residenzstätte Berlin und Potsdam*, Berlin 1769.

Noldus, Vera Badeloch, *Trade in Good Taste: Relations in Architecture and Culture between the Dutch Republic and the Baltic World in the Seventeenth Century*, Turnhout 2004.

Noldus, Vera Badeloch & Juliette Roding (eds.), *Peter Isaacsz (1568–1625): Court Painter, Art Dealer and Spy*, Turnhout 2007.

Nørregaard-Nielsen, Hans Edvard, "Borgen bliver slot," in: Hans Edvard Nørregaard-Nielsen et al. (eds.), *Danmarks Arkitektur. Magtens bolig*, Copenhagen 1980, 32–37.

Oechelhaeuser, Adolf von, *Das Heidelberger Schloss*, Heidelberg 1923.

Olden Jørgensen, Sebastian, "Hofkultur, ritual og politik i Danmark 1536–1746," in: Ulrik Langen (ed.), *Ritualernes Magt*, Copenhagen 2002, 47–75.

Olden Jørgensen, Sebastian, "State Ceremonial, Court Culture and Political Power in Early Modern Denmark 1536–1746," *Scandinavian Journal of History* 27 (2002) 65–76.

Olden Jørgensen, Sebastian, "Sommerstuen, Slotskirken og Dansesalen," in: Heiberg 2006, 115–31.

Olden Jørgensen, Sebastian, "Court Culture during the Reign of Christian IV," in: Noldus & Roding 2007, 15–30.

Ottenheym, Konrad, Paul Rosenberg & Niek Smit (eds.), *Hendrick de Keyser: Architectura Moderna. Moderne bouwkunst in Amsterdam 1600–1625*, Amsterdam 2008.

Ottenheym, Konrad, "Hendrick de Keyser and Denmark," in: Andersen, Bøggild Johannsen & Johannsen 2011, 313–24.

Ottenheym, Konrad, "Sculptors' Architecture: The International Scope of Cornelis Floris and Hendrick de Keyser," in: Ottenheym & Jonge 2013, 103–27.

Ottenheym, Konrad & Krista De Jonge, "Civic Prestige: Building the City 1580–1700," in: Krista De Jonge & Konrad Ottenheym (eds.), *Unity and Discontinuity: Architectural Relationships between the Southern and Northern Low Countries (1530–1700)*, Turnhout 2007, 209–50.

Ottenheym, Konrad & Krista De Jonge (eds.), *The Low Countries at the Crossroads: Netherlandish Architecture as an Export Product in Early Modern Europe (1480–1680)*, Turnhout 2013.

Paulson, Thomas, *Scandinavian Architecture: Buildings and Society in Denmark, Finland, Norway, and Sweden from the Iron Age until Today*, London 1958.

Peschken, Goerd & Hans-Werner Klünner (eds.), *Das Berliner Schloss*, Berlin 1982.

Peyton, Edward, *The Divine Catastrophe of the Kingly Family of the House of Stuarts*, London 1652.

Pontoppidan, Erik, *Den danske Atlas*, vol. II, Copenhagen 1764.

Randsborg, Klavs, "Inigo Jones & Christian IV: Archaeological Encounters in Architecture," *Acta Archaeologica* 75 (2004) 3–98.

Rasbech, Johan Peter, *Frederiksborg Slots Beskrivelse*, Copenhagen 1832.

Rathgeben, Frederik Jacob, *Wa(h)rhaffte Beschreibung zweyer Raisen, welcher erste (die Badenfahrt genannt) … Friedrich Hertzog zu Württemberg uund Teck … im Jahr 1592 von Mümppelgart aus in … Engellandt … verrichtet …*, Tübingen 1603.

Reid, Janet, *The Oxford Guide to Classical Mythology in the Arts 1300–1990*, vol. I–II, Oxford 1993.

Reindel, Ulrik, *Kronborgtapeterne. Pragt & Propaganda på Frederik II's Kronborg,* Copenhagen 2009.

Reindel, Ulrik, "The King Tapestries at Kronborg Castle: A "Mirror of Princes" for a Protestant Prince," in: Philippe Bordes & Pascal-François Bertrand (eds.), *Portrait et Tapisserie*, Turnhout 2015, 71–86.

Roberts 1606a = Henry Roberts, *The most royall and honourable entertainment of … Christiern the fourth, King of Denmarke*, London 1606 = Nichols 1828, vol. II, 54–69.

Roberts 1606b = Henry Roberts, *England's Farewell to Christian the Fourth, famous king of Denmarke: With a relation of such shewes & severall pastimes presented to his Miestie*, London 1606 = Nichols 1828, vol. II, 75–85.

Roding, Juliette, *Christiaan IV van Denemarken (1588–1648). Architectuur en stedebouw van een Luthers vorst*, Alkmaar 1991.

Roding, Juliette, "The Copenhagen Exchange (1619–1624) Designed by the Van Steenwinckel Brothers: 'Not for the secret arts of Mercury and Laverna …,'" in: Konrad Ottenheym, Krista De Jonge & Monique Chatenet (eds.), *Public Buildings in Early Modern Europe*, Turnhout 2010, 241–48.

Rosenthal, Earl, "*Plus ultra, non plus ultra,* and the Columnar Device of Emperor Charles V," *Journal of the Warburg and Courtauld Institutes* 34 (1971) 204–228.

Rye, William B., *England as seen by Foreigners in the Days of Elizabeth & James the First*, London 1865.

Schepelern, Henrik Ditlev, "Christian den Fjerde som Bygmester. Nogle Tanker omkring Porttaarnet paa Frederiksborg," *Kulturminder* 3. rk. bd. 1, 1973, 28–48.

Schmitz-von Ledebur, Katja, *Die Planeten und ihre Kinder. Eine Brüsseler Tapisserienserie des 16. Jahrhunderts aus der Sammlung Albrechts V. in München*, Turnhout 2009.

Schnitzer, Claudia, *Constellatio Felix – die Planetenfeste Augusts des Starken anlässlich der Vermählung seines Sohnes Friedrich August mit der Kaisertochter Maria Josepha 1719 in Dresden*, Dresden 2014.

Scholten, Fritz et al. (eds.), *Adriaen de Vries 1556–1626*, Cat. Amsterdam, Zwolle 1998.

Shapiro, James, *1606. William Shakespeare and the Year of Lear*, London 2015.

Skougaard, Mette, "Interiører," in: Heiberg 2006, 63–79.

Skovgaard, Joakim A., *A King's Architecture: Christian IV and his Buildings*, London 1973.

Slange, Niels, *Den Stormægtigste Konges Christian den Fierdes … Historie*, Copenhagen 1749.

Smith, Claus M., "Christian 4. som bygherre," in: Heiberg 2006, 261–83.

Spohr, Arne, "'This Charming Invention Created by the King': Christian IV and His Invisible Music," *Danish Yearbook of Musicology* 39 (2012) 13–33.

Steenberg, Jan, *Christian IVs Frederiksborg. Arkitektur, Interiører, Situationer,* Hillerød 1950.

Stein, Meir, "The Iconography of the Marble Gallery at Frederiksborg Palace," *Journal of the Warburg and Courtauld Institutes* 35 (1972) 284–293 (re-edited in Danish in: Stein 1987, 109–121).

Stein, Meir, *Christian den Fjerdes Billedverden*, Copenhagen 1987.

Strong, Roy, *The Renaissance Garden in England*, London 1979.

Stupperich, Reinhard, "Die zwölf Caesaren Suetons. Zur Verwendung von Kaiserporträt-Galerien in der Neuzeit," *Mannheimer Historische Forschungen* 6, Mannheim 1995, 39–58.

Summerson, John, "The Building of Theobalds, 1564–1585," *Archaeologia* 97 (1959) 7–26.

Summerson, John, *Architecture in Britain 1530–1830,* Yale 1993.

Sutton, James M., *Materializing Space at an Early Modern Prodigy House: The Cecils at Theobalds, 1564–1607*, Aldershot 2004.

Syndram, Dirk, *Das Schloss zu Dresden: von der Residenz zum Museum*, Leipzig 2012.

Thorlacius-Ussing, Viggo, "Billedhuggerkunsten," in: Knud Fabricius et al. (eds.), *Holland Danmark* II, Copenhagen 1945, 62–126.

Thurah, Lauritz, *Den Danske Vitruvius* II, Copenhagen 1749.

Thurley, Simon, *The Royal Palaces of Tudor England: Architecture and Court Life 1460–1547,* New Haven 1993.

Thurley, Simon, *Whitehall Palace: An Architectural History of the Royal Apartments, 1240–1698*, New Haven & London 1999.

Thurley, Simon, *Somerset House: The Palace of England's Queens 1551–1692*, London 2009.

Thurley, Simon, "The Historiography of the Architecture of European Courts," in: Marcello Fantoni (ed.), *The Court in Europe*, Rome 2012, 291–302.

Thurley, Simon, *The Building of England: How the History of England has Shaped our Buildings*, London 2013.

Thurley, Simon, *Houses of Power: The Places that Shaped the Tudor World*, London 2017.

Veldman, Ilja M., *Leerrijke reeksen van Maarten van Heemskerck*, Hague & Haarlem 1986.

Velte, Maria, *Die Anwendung der Quadratur und Triangulatur bei der Grund- und Aufrissgestaltung der gothischen Kirchen*, Basel 1951.

de Vries, Dirk J., "Uit de schaduw van Hendrick de Keyser. Gerrit Lambertsen van Cuilenborch (1597–1657), beeldhouwer en bouwmeister," *Bulletin KNOB* 115 (2016) 57–79.

de Vrigny, Jacques Philippe de la Combe, *Relation en forme de journal d'un voyage fait en Dannemarc*, Rotterdam 1706.

Wade, Mara R., *Triumphus nuptialis Danicus: German Court Culture and Denmark*, Wiesbaden 1996.

Wade, Mara R. (ed.), *Pomp, Power, and Politics: Essays on German and Scandinavian Court Culture and their Contexts,* in: *Daphnis* 32, 1–2 (2003).

Wade 2003a = Mara R. Wade, "The Queen's Courts: Anna of Denmark and her Royal Sisters: Cultural Agency at Four Northern European Courts in the Sixteenth and Seventeenth Centuries," in: Clare McManus (ed.), *Women and Culture at the Courts of the Stuart Queens*, Basingstoke 2003, 49–80.

Wanscher, Vilhelm, *Christian 4.s Bygninger*, Copenhagen 1937.

Warburg Institute, Iconographic Database at: https://warburg.sas.ac.uk/special-collections/photographic-collection/iconographic-database.

Watanabe-O'Kelly, Helen, *Triumphal Shews: Tournaments at German-Speaking Courts in their European Context 1560–1730*, Berlin 1992.

Watanabe-O'Kelly, Helen, *Court Culture in Dresden: From Renaissance to Baroque*, London 2002.

Weilbach, Frederik, *Frederiksborg Slot*, Copenhagen 1923.

Weilbach, Frederik, "Judicerhuset ved Frederiksborg Slot. En Berigtigelse," *Fra Frederiksborgs Amt* 1929, 74–76.

Weingart, Ralf, "Der Neubau des Güstrower Schlosses durch Franz Parr – 'wider die allte form, mass und gestalt'," in: Kornelia von Berswordt-Wallrabe (ed.), *Schloss Güstrow. Prestige und Kunst 1556–1636*, Güstrow 2006, 15–21.

Wiggins, Martin & Catherine Richardson (eds.), *British Drama 1533–1642: A Catalogue*, vol. v: *1603–1608*, Oxford 2015.

Wolf, Jens Lauritsøn, *Encomion regni Daniae*, Copenhagen 1654.

Young, Alan, *Tudor and Jacobean Tournaments*, London 1987.

Summary in Danish

Denne bog omhandler den af eftertiden glemte, indre sammenhæng og oprindelige betydning af Frederiksborgs meget omfattende skulpturudsmykning, hvoraf størstedelen i dag er gået tabt. Til udsmykningen af slottets facader blev der i 1600-tallets første årtier fra Prag og Amsterdam hjemskrevet mere end 60 skulpturer i bronze eller sandsten. Intetsteds i Norden var der en tilsvarende overdådig udsmykning.

Eftertidens restaureringer – særligt arkitekt Ferdinand Meldahls restaurering efter slotsbranden i 1859 – har grundlæggende forvansket slottets store, betydningsbærende billedprogram. Den hidtidige forsknings fokus har været på Slotskirken og på forgårdens Neptunfontæne, mens udsmykningen af Marmorgalleriet (1619–22) og Ridebanen (1615) har været stedmoderligt behandlet.

Med udgangspunkt i de bevarede elementer, hidtil upåagtede eller fejltolkede kilder fra samtiden samt 1600-tallets antikbaserede billedsprog rekonstrueres Marmorgalleriets og den indre slotsgårds tilgrundliggende billedprogram. Reliefudsmykninger med portrætter af forhistoriske konger af Danmark og den romerske historiker Suetons tolv romerske kejsere prydede vinduernes pedimenter. Guder og helte flankerede oprindelig kongens trappetårn, mens gudinder flankerede dronningens. Øverst, på toppen af galleriets syv øvre bueslag, stod helfigursskulpturer af de syv planetguder, hvis oprindelige placering, med Jupiter i midten, også påvises.

På Ridebanen er et af bogens fokuspunkter det af Ferdinand Meldahl nedrevne og af eftertiden glemte Dommerhus, der fra 1615 lige indtil 1865 (altså seks år efter branden) afsluttede Ridebanen mod syd. Her, omkring dette sørgeligt tabte Dommerhus og Ridebanens oprindelige skulpturudsmykning, kan anlægget vises at være associativt relateret til ringridningsbanen over dem alle, det romerske *Circus Maximus* for foden af kejserpaladset på Palatinerhøjen i Rom. Det var i denne optik et genskabt *Circus Maximus*, som man ved ringridningsdysterne så ned på fra vinduerne i slottets Audienshus, Løngang, Slotskirke og Riddersal. Ambitionerne var store – og viljen til at give dem visuelt udtryk ligeså.

Bogens andet fokus er den oversete indflydelse, som Christian IV's besøg i Dresden i 1597 og især England i 1606 fik for slotsanlæggets arkitektoniske udformning, såvel i de enkelte afsnit som i dets helhed.

Som noget ganske nyt tilskrives Christian IV's besøg i juli 1606 på det legendariske, siden ødelagte, paladsanlæg Theobalds en helt afgørende betydning for den derefter gennemførte udvidelse af Frederiksborg. Theobalds blev bygget midt i 1500-tallet af den magtfulde Cecil-familie som tilbagevendende residens for dronning Elizabeth I og blev siden overtaget af Stuart-kongerne som deres foretrukne residens. Efter Stuart-dynastiets fald blev slottet revet ned til grunden, hvilket forklarer, at kendskabet til det i dag er mangelfuldt. Men der vides nok til, at man kan se de åbenbare lighedspunkter med netop Frederiksborg.

Efter kongens hjemkomst i september 1606 kan det på Frederiksborg f.eks. iagttages, at der lægges en ny vægt på slottets symmetriakse, på en aksial adgangsrute, der fra den såkaldte S-bro og frem mod kongefløjens hovedfacade grupperer (næsten) alle arkitekturelementer omkring den centrale synsakse. Man har i denne sammenhæng altid talt om fransk påvirkning (særligt fra bygmesteren Jacques Androuët du Cerceaus berømte og ofte udgivne arkitekturtraktater) – hvad der i sidste ende sikkert er korrekt. Men man har overset, at Christian IV, der ligesom sine bygmestre aldrig var i Frankrig, fire dage i sommeren 1606 var gæst på et palads anlagt efter præcis disse principper, nemlig Cecil-familiens slot, Theobalds, hvis synsakse over godt 400 meter førte gennem to slotsgårde direkte frem mod hovedfacaden. Flere træk indikerer, at det var her, kongen hentede inspiration til det moderne, i sidste ende franskinspirerede helhedskoncept, der fra 1606 og frem bliver omsat i sandsten og tegl på Frederiksborg.

Det nye eftertryk på symmetri og aksialitet efterlod kongen og hans bygmestre med et akut facadeproblem. Den før 1606 fuldførte kongefløj savner – som man trods Meldahls modererende (om man vil: forfalskende) indgreb fortsat kan se – fuldstændig den regelbundne symmetri, som hele den nye, aksiale adgangsrute forudsatte skulle være "kronen på værket".

Frederiksborgs oprindelige kongefløjsfacade er på bedste middelalderlige facon bygget indefra og ud, præcis som det gamle Københavns Slot og Kongefløjen på faderens Kronborg. Christian IV's Frederiksborg havde ingen central og monumental indgangsportal og ingen symmetri i dispositionen af facadens vinduer. Et forhold, som den nye understregning af symmetriaksen pinligt ville eksponere.

Også på dette punkt tilbød Theobalds en løsning. Til sin pragtfacade havde Lord Cecil i 1580 hjemskrevet et toetages marmorgalleri fra Nederlandene. I 1619, ved afslutningen af byggeprocessen, gjorde Christian IV det samme – og med dette toetages galleris syv symmetriske bueslag er der, som en foranstillet *frons scaenae*, skabt en så skuffende illusion om en centralaksial facade, at moderne arkitekturhistorikere forbløffes, når de får eftervist den oprindelige asymmetri, der her er blevet kamufleret.

Slottets bygningshistorie er gennem påvisningen af denne engelske forbindelse blevet tilført en dynamik, der afdækker Frederiksborgs position som et dansk arkitekturhistorisk vendepunkt i 1600-tallets overgang til en ny, mere internationalt orienteret byggestil.

Index of Places, Monuments and Persons

Alessandro Farnese, Duke of Parma and Piacenza: 114, fig. 6.5
Anna, Princess of Denmark and Electress of Saxony: fig. 7.19
Anna Katherina of Brandenburg, Queen of Denmark & Norway: fig. 2.7
Anne, Queen of England & Scotland: 52, 119, 142, 153–55, 196, fig. 7.19, 7.30
Atalanta & Hippomenes: 57–58, fig. 3.17

Bagnacavallo, Bartolommeo (Ramenghi): 159, fig. 7.33
Baratta, Lazarus: fig. 2.1
Berg, Johan Adam: 71, 82, 98, 126, 133, fig. 1.5, 4.7
Berlin
    The *Schloss*: 129, fig. 2.3
    the *Stechbahn* at the castle: 127, 132–33, 141–42, 146, fig. 7.8
Beust, Heinrich: fig. 7.7
Bray, Salomon de: 87, 90, 93–94, 98–99, 106, 110, fig. 5.3
Bruun, Johann Jacob: fig. 8.4

Caus, Salomon de: 154–55, fig. 7.30
Cecil, Robert, Earl of Salisbury: 41–42, 45–46, 51, 67, 70, 194–95, fig. 3.8
Cerceau, Jacques Androuet du: 41, 43, 45–46, 52, 66, 70, 194, fig. 3.7
    Charleval: fig. 3.9
Charles IX, King of France: 45, fig. 3.9
Charles V, Habsburg Emperor: 26, 114, fig. 2.6
Christian I, Elector of Saxony: 129, fig. 7.23

Christian I, King of Denmark & Norway: fig. 7.4
Christian III, King of Denmark & Norway: 123
Christian IV, King of Denmark & Norway, passim
Christian V, King of Denmark & Norway: fig. 7.4
Christian VI, King of Denmark & Norway: 134, fig. 1.1, 5.10, 8.4
Christian VIII, King of Denmark: fig. 8.5
Clausen, Samuel: fig. 1.3
Cole, Emily: 118, 120, fig. 3.8
Compenius, Essias: fig. 8.3
Consus, see: Fredriksborg, *Neptune*
Copenhagen
    Christiansborg Palace: fig. 1.1
    Castle of Copenhagen: 36, 66
    The Blue Tower: 36
    The Exchange: 49
    Tiltyard at Castle: 127, 133, 146, fig. 7.9
    Tøjhuset: 52, fig. 3.13

Danckerts, Cornelis I.: 93
    planet-god prints after de Keyser: fig. 5.4
    sea-god prints after de Keyser: fig. 5.7
Danckerts, Justus
    planet-god prints after de Keyser: fig. 5.5
Dietterlin, Wendel: 22, 151, 153, fig. 7.27
Dowland, John: 153
Dresden: 17, 49, 194
    Der lange Gang: 121, 126, 142, 144–45, fig. 7.12, 7.21, 7.23
    Gallery of the *Schlosshof*: 68–69, fig. 4.6

Georgenbau: 121
Nosseni's bronze pillars: 133, 146, 148, 151, fig. 7.12, 7.21, 7.23
Pherdeschwemme: 141, fig. 7.12
Turnierhof: 127, 129–30, 133, fig. 7.12, 7.23
Zeughaus: 49–50, fig. 3.12
Drottningholm Palace: 23, fig. 3.10

Elizabeth I, Queen of England: 14, 42, 48–49, 120, 194
Erasmus Laetus: 14

Fehling, Carl Heinrich Jacob: fig. 7.21
Fincke, Caspar: 148, fig. 7.7, 7.24
Florence
   Palazzo Pitti: 96
Frederik II, King of Denmark & Norway: 14, 33, 163, fig. 1.1, 1.4, 4.5
Frederiksborg Castle: passim
   Absence of an original masterplan: 17, 38–39, 66
   Alexander the Great: 26, fig. 2.5
   Apollo (*Sol*), the planet-god: 96, 98, 100, 110, chariot of: fig. 5.5–6, 5.9
   Atalanta & Hippomenes: 57–58, fig. 3.17
   Audience House: 84, 115, 119, 121, 124, 133–34, 140, 142, 145, 153, 157, 167, fig. 7.2–4, 7.20, 7.22, 7.28, 7.29, 7.31
   Augustus, Roman emperor: 174n11
   Caligula, Roman emperor: 174n11
   Claudius, Roman emperor: 174n11
   Consus in the Tiltyard: 151, fig. 7.25
   Dan, legendary first King of Denmark: 75, fig. 1.4, 4.11
   Diana and Actaeon (here identified as), fountain in the park of: 153
   Diana (*Luna*), the planet-goddess: 91, 96, 100, 110–11, chariot of: fig. 4.15, 5.4, 5.6
   Domitian, Roman emperor: 72, 174n11
   Facade of Royal Wing
      as built in 1606: 62, 68, 142, fig. 4.3, 4.8, 4.14
      as restored by Meldahl: fig. 4.4, 4.14
   Forecourt: 17, 22, 25, 35–36, 38, 46, 53, fig. 1.5–6, 2.2, 2.5
   Fountain of Neptune: 22–24, 36–37, 112–14, 148, 151, fig. 2.2
   Galba, Roman emperor: 73, 174n11
   Gateway Tower: 22, 36–37, fig. 3.16
   Great Hall: 34, 59, fig. 3.4, 3.18
   Judicirhaus: 131, 133–34, 137, 140–42, fig. 7.13–18
   Julius Caesar: 26–27, 174n11, fig. 2.5, 4.7
   Jupiter, the planet-god: 101, 103, 107, ch. VI, passim, fig. 5.3, 5.14, 5.18, chariot of: 5.5–6
   Loggia: 37, 53, 59, fig. 3.16
   Marble Gallery: ch. IV–VI, passim, fig. 4.1–2, 4.14–15
   Mars & Venus relief: 157–59, fig. 7.31
   Mars, the planet-god: 95–96, 98, 100, 110, chariot of: fig. 5.5, 5.6
   Mercury, the planet-god: 95–96, 100, 111, chariot of: fig. 5.4, 5.6
   Minerva & the Muses statues: 151–57, fig. 7.28
   Neptune in the Tiltyard: 148–51, fig. 7.25
   Castle Chapel: 33–35, 49, fig. 3.11
   Pre-fire drawings, watercolours and photographs: fig. 7.2, 7.13, 7.15–18, 7.20
   Privy Gallery: 118–24, fig. 7.2–3, 7.5
   S-Bridge: 36–37, fig. 1.5–6, 3.5
   Saturn, the planet-god: 100, fig. 5.12–13, chariot of: fig. 5.3, 6.1, 6.3
   Terrace: ch. II and III, passim
      as originally built: fig. 3.2
      as redesigned by Steenwinckel: fig. 2.5, 3.14
   Tiberius, Roman emperor: 174n11
   Tiltyard: ch. VII, passim, fig. 7.13–18
      Arch: 146–51, fig. 1.5, 7.5, 7.7, 7.24–25
      Obelisks: 126, 148, 151
   Twelve gods and heroes on the Terrace facade: fig. 3.14
   Twelve gods and heroes on the Marble Gallery: fig. 4.1–2
   Venus & Cupid Fountain: 46, 62, fig. 3.10
   Venus, the planet-goddess (here identified as): 91, 96, 98, 105–6, fig. 5.2, 5.9,, chariot of: 5.5–6
   Vitellius, Roman emperor: 73, 174n11
Friis, Cristen: 14

Galle, Philips: fig. 6.5
Gercken, Didrick: fig. 7.24
Gertner, Johan Vilhelm: fig. 8.5
Goltzius, Hubert: 158–59, fig. 7.32
Grubbe, Sigvard: fig. 7.26
Güstrow, Palace of the Dukes of Mecklenburg
    Duke Ulrich's lodgings: 123
    Loggia: 68, fig. 5.1

Hansen, Heinrich: fig. 3.18
Harington, John: 48
Holm, Heinrich Gustav Ferdinand
    watercolour of the *Judicirhaus* at Frederiksborg: 138, fig. 7.16

Isaacsz, Pieter: fig. 1.2, 3.2, 8.6

James I, King of England and Scotland: 41, 42, 48, 52
Johann Georg, Elector of Brandenburg, Duke of Prussia: 129
Johannsen, Hugo: 35
Jones, Inigo: 47, 121, fig. 7.19
Jonghelinck, Jacques: 113–15, fig. 6.5

Keyser, Hendrick de: 13, ch. IV, passim, fig. 5.2
    Chariot of Mars: 95–96, 98, 110, fig. 5.5, 6.2
    Chariot of Saturn: 96, 110–11, fig. 5.4–5, 6.3
    City Hall of Delft: 70
    Exchange in Amsterdam: fig. 3.16
    Gallery at Frederiksborg: ch. IV, passim
    Hercules: 84, fig. 4.16
    Jupiter: 101, 103, 107, ch. VI, passim, fig. 5.3, 5.14, 5.18
    planet-god reliefs: ch. V–VI, passim, fig. 5.3, 5.6, 5.18, 6.2–3
    planet-god statues: ch. V–VI, passim, fig. 5.3, 5.9, 5.12–16, 5.18
    Saturn: 100, fig. 5.12
    Venus (here identified as): 91, 100, 103–6, fig. 5.3, 5.15–16
Knieper, Hans: fig. 1.4
Kronborg: 33, 66, 194, fig. 1.4, 4.5, 7.19, 8.6
Krøyer, Peter Severin: fig. 4.13

Lambertsen van Cuylenburg, Gerrit: 70, fig. 4.16, 5.12, 5.14–17, 6.2–3
London (and environs)
    Greenwich Palace: 49, 125, 133
    Nonsuch Palace: 55, 85
    Richmond Palace: 49, 120
    Royal Exchange: 48–49, fig. 3.16
    Somerset House
        Fountain in garden: 154–55, fig. 7.30
        Privy Gallery: 119
    Westminster Abbey: 49
    Whitehall Palace: 49
        Holbein Gate: 120
        Privy Gallery: 120
        Tiltyard: 120
Lorck, Melchior: fig. 1.1
Lund, Frederik Christian
    pre-fire drawings of Frederiksborg: 178n30, fig. 5.18, 7.18
Luther, Martin: 34
Lyngby, Thomas: 100

Magdalena Sibylla, princess of Saxony: fig. 7.11
Malmøhus Palace: 123
Mander, Karel van: fig. 3.15
Margrethe I, Queen of Denmark, Norway and Sweden: 14
Meldahl, Ferdinand: 71, 73, 76–80, 84, 106, 134, 139–40, fig. 3.4, 3.6, 4.3–4, 4.13–15, 5.9, 7.13
Moritz, Elector of Saxony: 69, fig. 4.6

Neurdenburg, Elisabeth: 93, 100
Nosseni, Giovanni Maria: 35, 129–30, 146, 148, fig. 7.9, 7.12, 7.21, 7.23

Osserjan, Gert: fig. 7.10
Ovid(-ius) Naso, Publius
    motifs from the *Metamorphoses*: 151–52, 173n36, fig. 3.17, 7.27–28

Paesschen, Hendrik van: 47–48
Panvinio, Onofrio: 151, fig. 7.26

Parr, Franz: fig. 5.1
Passe, Chrispijn de: fig. 7.11
Pedersen, Mogens: 153
Peters, Christian Carl: 79, fig. 2.5

Quellinus I, Artus: fig. 5.13

Reiman, Hans: 36
Resen, Peder Hansen: 126–27, 133, 150, fig. 7.6
Richardt, Ferdinand: fig. 4.12
Roed, Jørgen
    painting of the Frederiksborg Tiltyard: 137, 139, fig. 7.15
Rome
    Circus Maximus: 150, 194, fig. 7.23, 7.26
    Imperial Palace: 194
    Obelisks: 126, 146, 148, 151, fig. 7.23, 7.26
    Trojan Games: 150

Schütz, Heinrich: 153
Scipio Africanus: fig. 7.11
Scipio Asiaticus: fig. 7.11
Shakespeare, William: 48, fig. 7.19
Shapiro, James: 48
Sixtus V, pope: 151
Skovgaard, Peter Christian: 144, fig. 7.20
Somer, Paul van: fig. 7.19
Steenwinckel the Elder, Hans van: 41
Steenwinckel the Younger, Hans van: 13, 36–37, 41, 53–54, 66, ch. IV, passim, 88, 90–1, 98, 100, 110–12, 146, 148, 151, 157, fig. 3.2, 3.10, 3.15–16, 5.3, 6.4, 7.24, 7.27

Steenwinckel, Laurens van: 158–59, fig. 7.3, 7.28–29
Stein, Meir: 42, 94, 100, 158
Strong, Roy: 155
Suetonius Tranquillus, Caius: 74, fig. 4.7
Summerson, John: 42
Swenckius, Christophorus: fig. 7.11
Sweys (Sweis), Lorentz: 80

Theobalds: ch. III, passim, fig. 3.8
    Du Cerceau-inspired plan: 46, 66, fig. 3.7–9
    Gateway: 47
    projecting gallery range: 120, fig. 3.8
    Stone Gallery: 47–48, 67–69, fig. 3.8
    Venus & Cupid fountain: 42, 46
Thurah, Lauritz: 82, 99–103, 105–6, 148, fig. 4.3, 4.5, 5.10–11
Thurley, Simon: 119
Timm, Reinhold: fig. 8.1
Torgau
    Chapel: 34

Ulrich, Duke of Mecklenburg: 123, fig. 5.1

Versailles: 96
Vries, Adriaen de: 13, 22, 36, 76, 112–13, 148, fig. 2.2
Vries, Hans Vredeman de: 22

Windsor
    St George's Chapel: 49
    Order of the Garter: fig. 3.1
Winstrup, Laurits Albert: fig. 4.8
Wulff, Jørgen: fig. 3.10

Image Credits

Fig. 2.3; 3.12; 3.17; 5.1; 5.2; 6.1; 7.8; 7.23: AKG.

Fig. 3.8: Allan Adams © Historic England. Reproduced with generous permission by Dr Emily Cole and her colleagues at Historic England.

Fig. 3.18; 7.19: Bridgeman Images.

Fig. 8.1: The Danish Music Museum, Copenhagen – Musikhistorisk Museum & The Carl Claudius Collection.

Fig. 1.6; 3.5: Dansk Drone Inspektion Aps.

Fig. 2.1: Gripsholm Castle, Sweden. Public domain.

Fig. 2.4: © Grünes Gewölbe, Staatliche Kunstsammlungen, Dresden. Jürgen Karpinski.

Fig. 4.4 and 7.25: © Kirsten Marie Kragelund.

Fig. 1.2; 2.2; 2.5; 3.2–4; 3.11; 3.14; 3.16; 4.2; 4.7; 4.9; 4.12; 4.16; 5.10; 5.12; 5.14–16; 7.7; 7.3–5; 7.15–6; 7.28; 7.31; 8.2–4: The Museum of National History at Frederiksborg. Photos of 2.2 and 7.3 are by Ole Haupt, 5.10 and 7.15 by Lennart Larsen, the rest by Kit Weiss.

Fig. 1.1; 4.13; 8.6: The National Gallery of Denmark. Public domain.

Fig. 1.4; 3.10; 3.13; 5.18; 7.17–8; 7.22: The National Museum of Denmark. Public domain.

Fig. 7.20: Ordrupgaard, Copenhagen. Pernille Klemp.

Fig. 5.4; 5.5; 5.7; 7.32: Rijksmuseum, Amsterdam. Public domain.

Fig. 1.3; 3.1; 3.15; 4.10; 7.1; 7.10; 8.5: The Royal Danish Collection, Rosenborg.

Fig. 2.6; 3.7; 3.9; 4.11; 7.6; 7.9; 7.11; 7.26–7; 7.30: The Royal Danish Library.

Fig. 4.1: The Royal Danish Library. © Keld Helmer-Petersen.

Fig. 1.5; 2.7; 3.6; 4.3; 4.5; 4.8–9; 4.14–5; 5.3; 5.6; 5.8–9; 5.11; 5.17; 6.2–4; 7.2; 7.8; 7.13–4; 7.24; 7.29: Danish National Art Library.

Fig. 4.6: Prof. Jörg Schöner, Dresden.

Fig. 7.33: Staatliche Graphische Sammlung, Munich.

Fig. 7.12: © Staatliche Kunstsammlungen, Dresden. Jürgen Karpinski.

Fig. 7.21: © Staatliche Kunstsammlungen, Dresden, Kupferstich-Kabinett. Herbert Boswank.

Fig. 6.5: © The Trustees of the British Museum, London.

Fig. 5.13: Wikimedia Commons.